A FORK ON THE ROAD

A FORK ON
THE ROAD

400
Cities
One
Stomach

Mark DeCarlo

GUILFORD, CONNECTICUT

An imprint of Globe Pequot Press

Dedication

This book would not have been possible if my mother the writer hadn't threatened to withhold Little League unless I took that Summer School typing class. Thanks, Angela Rocco DeCarlo.

To Yeni for changing her seat. Love to you being.

To buy books in quantity for corporate use
or incentives, call **(800) 962–0973**
or e-mail **premiums@GlobePequot.com.**

Lyons Press is an imprint of Globe Pequot Press.
Interior photos courtesy of Mark DeCarlo, unless otherwise credited.
Text design: Sheryl P. Kober
Project editor: Julie Marsh
Layout: Melissa Evarts

Library of Congress Cataloging-in-Publication Data
DeCarlo, Mark, 1962-
  A fork on the road : 400 cities/one stomach / Mark DeCarlo.
      p. cm.
  Includes bibliographical references and index.
  ISBN 978-0-7627-5140-2 (alk. paper)
  1. Food habits. I. Title.
  GT2850D43 2010
  394.1'2—dc22

Printed in the United States of America

10 9 8 7 6 5 4 3 2 1

Contents

FOREWORD: Cooking People

During four seasons hosting the Travel Channel program *Taste of America*, I logged more kitchen-hours than Poppin' Fresh, tasting four hundred unique and offbeat recipes. And every time I dropped something new into my mouth, I'd always wonder: "Who was the first guy to eat this?" Sometimes, as with blueberry pie, pizza, and deep-fried Snickers, it's obvious. But mostly I wondered how many favorite recipes were discovered on a dare.

Whether it's a bunch of hungry, moose-poor Eskimos slopping together whale blubber, frozen berries, and tuna and calling it fish ice cream, or old Italian women cramming pork butt, spices, and peppers into pig intestines and calling it sausage, every "food" was "discovered" by someone.

Consider the slimy, unopened oyster. If you didn't know it was hollow and contained a tasty glob of salty protein under that thick coating of green crap, would you ever guess that this rock was edible?

Well . . . somebody did. Deep in the recesses of time, some Neanderthal or beach-dwelling ape not only discovered that oysters aren't rocks . . . but that they're tasty—especially if you've got Tabasco and a date for the night. Maybe while striking two together to start a fire, maybe while throwing one to protest objectionable behavior, maybe during a percussion

> **No matter the dish, one thing is always true: the food—its taste, texture, and nutritional value—is always less interesting than the people preparing it. Especially in a drive-thru at 3:00 a.m.**

solo, eventually an oyster cracked open revealing its secret. At that moment, our inquisitive ancestor faced the pivotal question responsible for everything on Earth. The question, that in a very real way, defines who we are and what we will become:

"Should I put that in my mouth?"

Thankfully, for the bar owners on Bourbon Street, oysters were a "yes." But for every oyster success story, there are millions of casualties that will forever remain unknown. History is written by the people who live long enough to tell their friends about it.

A Fork on the Road celebrates those survivors and their progeny: It's about the kinds of people who will spend 30 percent of their yearly salary building a barbecue trailer with a homemade flaming logo painted on the side just to win a $50 contest five hundred miles from home. It's about the third generation pie maker who is as dull as a hammer until the conversation comes around to "cracker" versus "pastry" shells. It's about the millions of people around the country who used to refer to themselves as "cooking people," until the cannibals complained. Now, they prefer the deliciously more pretentious "foodies"—as if the rest of us exist simply on air, water, and *Family Guy* reruns.

I got lucky. The Travel Channel sent me to the right place at the right time: America, at the turbulent turn of a new century. The show told personal stories from people's houses, restaurants, and in some cases bedrooms. The resulting episodes reveal as much about the eaters as the eaten. But in a scant thirty minutes a week, the shows couldn't reveal everything. This book shares the best of the rest with you.

But this isn't a cookbook, really. Sure, there are plenty of delicious and idiosyncratic recipes, and the Web is stuffed with more. But food, alone on its plate, isn't all that interesting. It just sits there, waiting to become . . . well, us. (Unless it's lobster, in which case it makes a lame effort to escape. But how far could you get if your legs were rubber-banded together?) No, this book is about the people who do the cooking and the eating.

These strangers, many of whom became my friends, all wanted to celebrate their recipes—which usually weren't theirs at all, but belonged to a beloved aunt, grandmother, or uncle. They wanted to celebrate their people, by telling us new people about what they ate, why they ate it, and some of the best memories of when they all got together just to eat it.

I watched a grown man describe, through unrelenting tears, the flakey crust and just-sweet-enough texture of his momma's pecan pie. I got accused of bird-dogging a granny at a square dance, only to have tensions dissolved over juicy fried green tomatoes and Conway Twitty. And after three decades of enjoying from a safe distance, I finally dug into gooey squid guts to help prepare my Aunt Cookie's stuffed calamari on what would prove to be her final Christmas Eve.

Because of my travels, I've compiled a more authentic oral history of our American life and times than anyone you've ever met—unless you were personal friends with Charles Kuralt. *A Fork on the Road* is a travel memoir that celebrates America's most creative people through the foods they offer their guests. Because no matter the dish, one thing is always true: the food—its taste, texture, and nutritional value—is always less interesting than the people preparing it. Especially in a drive-thru at 3:00 a.m.

But who has the time to strike out across the continent and discover that kind of stuff these days, what with the Internet, drugstore sushi, and 24/7 *SportsCenter*?

I did.

So like a mommy bird, I've done all the flying, searching, and chewing for you . . . all you have to do is open up and enjoy the carefully chosen, tasty morsels as they're regurgitated across these cleverly designed pages.

Who's hungry?

Chapter 1
Rules of the Road

Starbucks, Applebee's, and Olive Garden are winning. More than ever before, Denver could be Dallas, and Atlanta looks like Louisville. The Creeping Beige dulls more purple mountain majesty each year, endeavoring to homogenize, standardize, and sanitize every mall, restaurant, and attraction in America. It's no accident that every Wal-Mart looks the same on the inside—its marketing synergy. Neighbors return from Rome crowing about how fantastic it was: "The McNuggets there taste just like the ones here!" Really? Passport revoked.

America's pot used to melt at a much slower rate. Before the late 1950s, cross-country road trips rolled over two lanes, not twelve. It took eighteen hours, a fuel stop, and plenty of cash to fly on a DC-3 from New York to Los Angeles. People lived and died pretty much where they were born, so regional idiosyncrasies, verbal and culinary, simmered undisturbed for generations. Because now many of those flavors are all but gone, my goal was to taste America, then share what I discovered, as honestly and humorously as possible.

We celebrated genuine people in their natural habitats, many of whom were entertainingly nuts. Like the teacher/football coach who spends weekends dressed up as the deceased "inventor" of the hamburger, preaching juicy epistles wherever two or more gather to grill. Or the guy who made his own

"Mr. Pierogi" costume. And the bald retiree who flounces around dressed as a "sexy" garlic bulb. To have this kind of fun, you gotta get off the couch. When was the last time the AARP sent a sexy garlic bulb to knock on your door?

Food is the story of civilization. Wars, nations, ideologies . . . everything happens, or doesn't, because of food. And it's been that way since the first farmer told his story on a cave wall.

"No more chase food that wants US for food! We can MAKE food with magic rocks. Put tiny rocks in mud by river, wait six moons, then Bang! Cornbread and rice cakes!"

Crops led to ranching, livestock to high-protein diets. Steaks made us stronger and bigger brained, which led to tools, art, big-screen TVs for cable shows about food, and charming, inquisitive hosts who stop and listen to every remotely interesting person they meet along the road. And ultimately, to this book of sometimes hilarious, always engaging stories, shaken and stirred-up from coast to coast. Follow my simple Ten Rules

of the Road to travel like you mean it, and start your own collection of people and places to remember. And do it quick . . . before there's no "there" there anymore.

RULE #1: GET OFF!

The only travel worth taking—especially in the "Full Body Search" Era—is authentic, unscripted adventure. That means no malls, no airport souvenir shopping, no cookie-cutter tours. If you're going to go through the effort of getting off the couch, get waaaaay off. Genuine "joints" are rarely located interstate-adjacent. Most restaurants along the twelve-lanes are corporate chains that know you'll be forty miles downwind before their grub starts to haunt you. Patronize places without a corporate headquarters—the food's tastier. It HAS to be, or they'd be gone.

You won't find these jewels at 55 MPH; you'll have to slow down and probably even wait at some stop signs. They're on U.S. routes, state highways, and Main Streets—America's real Adventure Trail. You can't smell the best biscuits in Tennessee from I-24 or I-40. Nope. To get within whiffing distance of the Loveless Café, you've got to be forty-five minutes outside of Nashville on Highway 100.

After that, just close your eyes and follow your nose. Miss Carol Fay always said she'd take her secret recipe to her grave.

Sadly, in early 2010, she did. But she must've whispered it to someone, because her oven still bakes them biscuits into the perfect Eulogy, fresh every hour of every day.

Yes it's a cliché, but take the dotted line less traveled. Yes, it will lengthen your trip. Yes, that can be a good thing.

RULE #2: LOCAL LOVE

Refuse the catchy siren call of franchised food. Yeah, I know you've got a gift card. Sure, the kids love the PlayLand, and yes, you know exactly what you're getting. That's exactly the problem.

Keep driving and enjoy the scenery, secure in the knowledge that no matter where you are, people get hungry. And thank God many of them would still rather eat at their friend's place, or the joint near the bowling alley, or even IN the alley instead of unwrapping their dinner in the driver's seat. Trust the Force.

Isn't that the best part of travel? Coming home to brag to your friends about the "great burger place" you found when your car hit a fiberglass ELK in Kentuckyanna and you had to kill an afternoon. Relating in exquisite detail every juicy morsel Craig—the owner's name was Craig—packed between his homemade sourdough cheese-toast. Making your friends feel bad they missed it is always the best dessert.

Every family is allowed one exception to the "no franchise" axiom. Mine is a guilty southern pleasure. There's  a calming effect Georgia's rolling pines confer over time. Boredom leads to irritation with the driver's music selection and eventually to wonder, typically a ninety-minute process, during which no fewer than twenty-eight Waffle Houses will zip past your windows, peeking out between the trees shrouding the interchanges.

Gathered around the chipped Formica counters and only slightly uncomfortable booths, southerners still practice the lively art of conversation.

Because the Waffle House is located in a region I just visit, it's my allowable indulgence. It's like a college sociology lab with bacon, the South's communal kitchen. Gathered around the chipped Formica counters and only slightly uncomfortable booths, southerners still practice the lively art of conversation. Polite to a fault, it's sometimes difficult to understand the difference between what they say and what they mean. Politics, NASCAR, doesn't matter what you talk about, they'll usually oblige with sweet, gentle responses. They might think you're a monumental idiot . . . but unlike New Yorkers, they'll try to hide it. You'll know it's time to go when a sultry lady says, "Well, Bless your heart!" That's the equivalent of a Queens plumber hitting you with a pipe. At that point, eat your last seven pieces of bacon and git.

RULE #3: A GOOD SIGN IS A GOOD SIGN

A great road sign says a lot about the place it's pimping: If mom and/or pop have a good sense of humor, even if the food stinks, at least you're guaranteed some yuks for dessert.

As a seasoned roadside reader, I've learned to extract hidden morsels of information that help guide me to the perfect stop via the billboard array that assaults your senses on the approach to

every
town of more
than five hundred.

GOOD SIGN: No area code, it means the joint's
been open forever, since the days when phone numbers were
seven digits long. The only reason a place in the middle of
nowhere stays open more than six months is good food.

GOOD SIGN: Battered, broken partially unreadable signs.
Call the number: If they answer, it's the best place around. (You
don't need to worry about your sign if you're always busy.) If the
number's changed and you're calling somebody's house, pretend
not to understand and start reciting a to go order. If you get
them to actually cook it for you, you've got talent.

RULE #4: LOCATION, LOCATION, LOCATION

Every town has its center, even if it's sometimes out in the woods.
As a traveler, it's your job to develop an inner fun-compass that
will, more often than not, point you in the right direction. It's a
combination of asking questions, reading before you roll, and

timing. Chicago in January is not the same place as Wrigley Field on the Fourth of July.

The neon sign for the Hotel Monteleone in New Orleans hangs on a side street, almost like it's hiding from the revelers in the Quarter. In style, color, and feel, it is perfect, down to the ancient Mardi Gras beads hanging from the A. Perhaps only the BATES MOTEL sign revealed more about the mojo lurking inside. On a street where even the ATMs have street barkers, the Monteleone doesn't chase. It waits around the corner from the carnival, knowing you'll eventually stumble down the right side street.

Beale Street in Memphis is a Main Street if ever there was one. Just a fried PB&B's toss from Graceland, Beale is three blocks of concentrated gris-gris and rib sauce, punctuated by authentic local music from bands like the incendiary Dempseys. The sign at the Rum Boogie Café doubles as the city's mantra.

I've been to Memphis many times, and yes, Beale is "touristy." But there's a reason—it's a deliciously authentic strip of musical heritage; like Broadway in Nashville, it features a near perfect blend of brews, blues, and barbecues. If you're within two hundred miles, go.

RULE #5: NO RERUNS

No matter how long you stay in a city, don't eat at the same place twice until you officially file your change of address form with the post office. Even one-horse towns have two diners. Yes, after a fantastic discovery, you will be tempted. But be strong. Traveling right means risking a bad meal now and then. It's the only way to find places like Gus's Fried Chicken down by the river in Memphis, and Buono's Beef way off the strip in Vegas. After a particularly succulent meal, compliment the owner and ask him or her to recommend their favorite eatery. Never fails.

RULE #6: TALK TO STRANGERS

In Los Angeles where I live, strangers literally jump when you talk to them . . . then they tell you about their screenplay. On the road, I always chat with food service people. They're usually tuned into the best places to eat and play. They come by this expertise because they all party together—starting with "happy hour" at 3:00 a.m. It's a sacred fraternity, and by virtue of the show I've been allowed in as a pledge. The most tangible benefit of this affiliation is tapping into the finely tuned palates of the local gastro-mafia everywhere we go. Now I'm sharing this secret handshake with you because you were savvy enough to buy this book . . . or skim it quickly in someone else's bathroom.

Other travelers can sometimes offer insights, but seek out the locals to get the unvarnished truth. Most people are proud of their town and delight in sharing tips with interested visitors.

The hard part is the approach—it's like picking up someone in a bar. I'm direct: "If you had one meal left before you die, and you had an ankle bracelet that prevented you from leaving this town, where would you go?" After a brief moment of staring, you can usually prod them into a conversation that will yield valuable intelligence. If they answer too quickly, discreetly check to see if, in fact, they ARE wearing a bracelet.

RULE #7: THE NAME OF THE GAME

Sometimes though, you walk into a town that looks like a *Twilight Zone* set—empty. When there's no one around to talk to, it means that all the fun people are somewhere else. It then becomes your job to find them . . . in order to enjoy them. Brian the Cameraman came up with a great game that guarantees a night of good food and atmosphere. As a tribute the game

is called Brian. As in, "Hey, let's play some Brian after work." (It's way better than playing Shooter, a game named after an erstwhile first-season audio guy. To play Shooter, you sit in the corner and smoke cigarettes until your girlfriend calls to tell you why you're an idiot.)

To play Brian in a strange town, head to a nearby bar for a cocktail. Sit only at the bar. Order one drink. When that drink is done, ask the person who physically placed the drinks in front of you to direct you to their favorite local place to eat. Then, no matter what they say, go. It will ALWAYS be good.

Brian is how we found Sodini's in San Francisco, Bob's Steak and Chop House in Dallas, and that great Thursday night blues show in Burlington, Vermont, with Buddy Guy, Dr. John, and Susan Tedeschi. After dinner, whoever drops the check is charged with selecting the next location. Brian ends when the meal or beverage is gone, and a unanimous vote certifies you are in a place too fun to leave. Make sure to use this same foolproof system to find your cabbie at the end of the night. You do not want to be arrested for DWB—Driving While Brianing.

RULE #8: NIGHTLIFE

Every city worth visiting has a best bar band, a musical hierarchy that transcends every barrier. There's always one gunslinger—it's your job to find him or her before you go wheels up.

In Dallas in the early 1980s, the gunslinger's name was Stevie Ray Vaughan. If you didn't live in Texas, you'd never heard of him . . . but if you did . . . you knew. Today, in cities like St. Louis, Memphis, and New Orleans, there are fantastic unknown musicians that will rock your world—difficult to find, but worth it.

Music is the most evocative regional flavor left in America, shorthand to the pulse of a city . . . or a crossroads in the middle of nowhere. Especially when you're going to be in town just a night or two, don't beige-out in the hotel bar listening to soulless music and checking your e-mail. To find your favorite music, no matter where you are, just play Captain Fun.

To play Captain Fun while traveling, start by looking around the bar, restaurant, or hotel lobby, to find the server who looks, acts, or sounds the most like you. The idea is to find your demographic match. The chances of a twenty-year-old girl and a sixty-year-old man going ape-shit over the same band are small, unless you're in West Hollywood. So, unlike Brian, Captain Fun requires some repetition.

> **To play Captain Fun while traveling, start by looking around the bar, restaurant, or hotel lobby, to find the server who looks, acts, or sounds the most like you.**

Say "Who's the best bar band in town and where are they playing tonight?" to as many demographically-correct servers/patrons as it takes to hear the same band three times. This weeds out people with weird musical tastes and shills with roommates in crappy cover bands.

Once three different people name the same band, you must go and listen until the end of one set. After that, you can stay or play Captain Fun again. If you never get three, the local music scene isn't worth the trouble. Just play Brian.

Am I a gunslinger? No, I'm a harmonica whore. Usually, I don't like getting recognized in public. But when I'm at a show with a band I dig, I can't be recognized enough. In a joint, booze

Bar Band

It's important to make sure people understand exactly what a bar band is: A bar band plays covers and originals. At least one member of a bar band must still have a day job. A bar band loads their own stage. The best bar bands make you forget about work, food, and how you're getting home. If you leave the joint shaking your head and wondering how come guys this good are playing in a dump like this, you've just seen a bar band.

COURTESY OF LIBBY KLEBECK

usually works. Between sets I'll order a round of drinks for the bar band, and have our server take it over, making sure that they mention it's from "that guy on TV." The band comes over to say thanks, we talk, I force an intern to mention that I play harmonica. Shameless but fun.

RULE #9: MORNING

Don't eat in your hotel, even if it's the Monteleone. Go out and find groggy locals or ornery waitresses and grab a seat. Sure, the temptation to just grab a cup of franchise coffee is strong. You're tired and cranky from playing Brian all night, and you got stuff to do and a nasty cup of java ain't gonna get it done. But be strong. Talk to some strangers, read a paper you never knew existed, and look around. A week from now you'll be miles away from here, but most of these folks will still be here. Figure out why before you leave.

RULE #10: WRITE IT DOWN

Pictures are great, but when you're on the road eight months a year, if you don't write stuff down, you wake up one day and half your life is lost in the haze of rental cars and hotel cardkeys.

Because I knew we were setting out to find great stories, and because I knew twenty-two minutes a week wouldn't scratch the surface, I started keeping notes on day one. I'd end every day typing random notes on my computer. After a month or so, I started skipping days and started promising myself I'd just remember stuff. To stay consistent, I needed someone to write to. In a moment of inspiration, I found him.

My dead dog, Groucho.

Groucho was always intensely interested in my solo adventures. Whenever I came home, whether from the store or the airport, he'd meet me at the door and sniff out everything he wanted to know. Then he'd look me over, sigh loudly, and climb up into my favorite chair to sit as if he were posing for a portrait.

My Favorite . . . SOUVENIR SHOPPING
Canal Street/Little Italy, New York City

Where else can you get a $4000 watch for $20? Where else can you get $10,000 engagement diamond rings for $50? Where else can you find "Kiss me, I'm Italian" shirts in XXXL?

South of Little Italy, Canal Street boasts—if that's the right word—more stands of cheap, Chinese imported crap than any two-block stretch in the country.

I always have to wear a watch. Don't feel dressed without one. But, I've had them stolen and broken on the road too often to wear my good ones on trips. The solution? Canal Street. I can get a great-looking watch for $20. Sure, it will literally fall apart, piece by piece after a few months, but so what? In the interim, it provides me with carefree wear and instant time updates whenever I need them.

Looking for faux jewelry, pashminas, sunglasses, or anything else made of plastic and shipped from far, far away? Look no further than Canal Street.

And if you walk the entire two-block stretch without finding something to spend your spare change on, keep walking past Chinatown to Little Italy where you're sure to find something funny to buy for the folks back home. Every cliché Italian shirt, hat, photo, or poster ever made is still on sale here at Garlic Central. Soccer jerseys, Godfather posters, Sopranos' cast albums, they got it all . . . 'cause they know a guy who can get it for you wholesale.

Then when you're done shopping, sit down and have a nice meal. Have some wine, relax, and enjoy yourself. Forgettabudit!

After 4,539 days of companionship, hilarity, and Frisbee catching, Groucho died two weeks before I started traveling for *Taste of America*.

Those first few weeks were the worst, but the act of writing Groucho letters cheered me for a few minutes a day while preserving specific memories of our trips. To be clear, while he was alive, Groucho could neither read nor write. Even so, telling him about our adventures was a great excuse to write it all down.

Without those letters, most of the people and places in this book would have receded past the point of accurate remembrance. So if you like this book, thank Groucho. If you don't, blame a cat.

Let's go for a ride!

BERT'S CHILI: WAFFLE HOUSE
The ULTIMATE Twenty-four Hour Roadside Driving Fuel

Bert began his career as a Waffle House restaurant manager in 1974. Since then, Bert has worked his way up to serve as president of the restaurant chain. While Bert is proud of his many responsibilities with Waffle House, he admits his claim to fame can be summed up in one word: "chili." Bert's Chili is served in over four million bowls every year.

1 pound lean hamburger

¼ pound breakfast sausage

2 cups chopped yellow onion

2 (15-ounce) cans pinto beans (not drained)

1 can (15 ounces) tomato sauce

2 cubes beef bouillon (or 2 tablespoons beef bouillon granules)

1 teaspoon salt

1 teaspoon chili powder

¾ teaspoon ground cumin

¼ teaspoon black pepper

¼ teaspoon sugar

⅛ teaspoon garlic powder

⅛ teaspoon ground oregano

1. Brown hamburger, sausage, and onions together in 6-quart saucepan.
2. Add pinto beans (not drained), add can of tomato sauce, and add enough water to rinse can.
3. Add beef bouillon granules. If using beef bouillon cubes, dissolve in ¼ cup water then add to the pan.

4. Add salt, black pepper, garlic powder, ground oregano, cumin, chili powder, and sugar. Blend thoroughly.
5. Bring to boil, reduce heat, and simmer for 15 minutes. Serve.

Get back in your car, drive.

COURTESY OF WAFFLE HOUSE INC.

Chapter 2
Coast to Coast

Travel is, by definition, an adventure. But not everyone is a traveler. A true traveler's need for being somewhere else is hardwired. My Aunt Cookie loved to travel; after seventy-eight action-packed years, her passport read like an atlas. Her father, not so much. He was eighty-five the day he took his first airplane ride, and afterwards, all he could talk about was the cashews . . . and the skirts on the waitresses.

Travel made us human. A mere sixty thousand years ago, early man figured out how to light his own torch, stood on two legs, and started walking north. We haven't stopped moving since. Deep inside the Great Pyramid, archaeologists recently discovered a mummified KFC bucket and a bathroom key chained to an oversize replica of the Sphinx, proving the migrations that birthed humanity into Europe and Asia coincided with advances in technology, brain size, and bargain travel packages through the Sinai. The curious, the hungry, the innovators: These were the adventure addicts who left the certainty of home to find . . . something else.

Think about that. Not as an anthropological concept, but about the specific individuals who did it.

Our hairy ancestors had absolutely no idea of what lay ahead in the darkness . . . none. They didn't even know they didn't know. Still, something made them get up and go. Maybe they were tired of getting eaten by lions. Maybe they'd had it with the heat. Or maybe, they just wanted to discover . . . if there were things to discover.

And every night along their journey they'd stop and gather around a fire their magician would somehow build—out of stone and trees. The roaring blaze would protect them through the night from hungry beasts and irritated locals, ensuring they'd be fed and rested if the sun decided to return to light the next chapter of their journey. No planes, trains, or automobiles, just handfuls of terrified pedestrians, hunkered around a blaze months from anyone or anything they knew. Every night, their stories would get longer and more astounding as they recounted the day's adventure. Ultimately ascending into the sky, like the smoke from the mystical light, these tales created a legend that drew even more fearless wanderers out along the route. Those ancient fires lit our communal spark for being somewhere else, someplace better.

And they're still burning today. The success of these intrepid thrill seekers ensured that the Travel Gene got passed on. Alexander, Marco Polo, Columbus, Ferdinand Magellan, Lewis & Clark, the Mercury Seven . . . we remember these guys because they had the best jobs around. Well that, and because they succeeded. Magellan's wasn't the first expedition to sail off around the world . . . they were just the first to come back.

> **Magellan's wasn't the first expedition to sail off around the world . . . they were just the first to come back.**

Today when we begin a trip, it's plotted and catalogued before we even leave the house. We know the weather for the foreseeable future and receive rewards for choosing the place from which we rent our GPS-equipped luxury motorcoach. We even see video of the place we'll sleep, in case the rigors of modern travel cause us to forget what a lamp and a desk look like. Our transportation is confirmed and the shuttle leaves every five minutes. Unlike the intrepid souls of old, today's road warriors plan their trade routes to ensure the least amount of novelty possible. As for me, I think it's much more fun to pay attention along the way.

Every airport's a stage, and all the men and women, merely players. Each three-letter acronym is filled with every make and model of human, all engaged in the high drama of getting where they're going without seeing where they're going. Lovers kiss goodbye at the curb; secretly dating coworkers clumsily help each other unpack their laptops for inspection. Mommies talk their kids off to school, and harried dads scan the cheesy airport souvenirs for something, anything that doesn't look like it came from an airport. Hordes of people, all going somewhere, murmuring to themselves like psychos. If you're tuned in, it's a helluva show.

If you were somehow teleported from 1995 into LAX on a random Monday morning in the present, you'd think you'd been dropped into an asylum. Gaggles of solitary people gesture and explain extremely important things . . . to no one. Lawyers negotiate wireless plea bargains while filling a urinal. Women stare at strangers and whisper suggestively, to someone a world away. The cellphone opera is especially irritating early in the morning when someone—usually a self-important guy wearing sunglasses inside the terminal—insists on broadcasting his opinions before the first flight of the day. Especially if you're try-

COURTESY OF LIBBY KLEBECK

ing to stay groggy until you can get on the plane and finish your dream.

It was 6:00 a.m. on a Monday in May when the bozo sitting next to me at LAX's Gate 43 got loud enough to wake me up. I tried going back to sleep, but it was impossible with the bullhorn blaring next to me. This was a job for Travel Avenger, defender of transit peace, inflictor of prankster justice.

To provide for the domestic travel tranquility of myself, and my mostly comatose neighbors, I started answering the loudmouth like I thought he was talking to me. As usual, at first I got the wave-off while he continued to announce "his awesome-est weekend ever" update to the entire terminal. Pretending not to understand, I responded louder, and got a more furtive wave-off. I was already gonna be awake for the whole flight, so nothing stopped me from shouting back at him that I don't remember spending any time with him this weekend. . . . Then it happened.

He covered his phone and barked the magic words, "I'm ON the PHONE!!"

"Well, the rest of us aren't," I bellowed in my gruffest Travel Avenger voice. "Keep it down."

I was rewarded with audible guffaws and Bozo's rapidly reddening face. My work was done. I grabbed Bozo's *People* magazine and pretended to care. A few minutes later, like clockwork, a grateful neighbor delivered me a "thank you" Starbucks. Thus began my new adventure.

We landed in Miami and packed into our rental for what I thought was a short trek across the Keys. What I didn't know is that we could have flown directly into Key West . . . for an additional $125. Instead, our frugal network had me brave a torturous land-bridge route that regularly washes out during hurricanes.

There are forty-two rickety, single-lane bridges along the route to Key West, evidently built out of Popsicle sticks and driftwood by conquistadors with a death wish.

I should point out, that for all my bluster about "adventure" and "intrepid wanderlust," I'm only referring to landlocked travel. The ocean is a totally different beast.

I was only five when I saw the *Titanic* sink like a black and white lead pipe on my grandparents' Zenith TV. On my first trip to the Pacific Ocean two years later, I was knocked around like a tubby cork with salty snot. In high school the Maui catamaran our family was on almost capsized

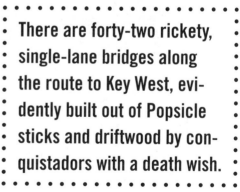

There are forty-two rickety, single-lane bridges along the route to Key West, evidently built out of Popsicle sticks and driftwood by conquistadors with a death wish.

on a snorkel excursion. At UCLA my nose was broken into three pieces while boogie boarding off the coast of LAX . . . on a topless beach, so I don't count that one.

Still, a lifetime of aquatic near-death experiences makes it impossible for me to spell "B-O-A-T" without getting sick. And now, I'd spend the next eight hours wobbling a watery tightrope over shark-infested waters. For cable money.

The tropical scenery was gorgeous, I'm told. From dusk into the night, we careened between oncoming traffic and certain death, teetering high above the ocean between forty-three dollops of dirt, just a well-timed gust away from becoming sashimi for some lucky shark. It was exhausting.

I gripped the armrest and kept watch for hurricanes, pirates, and/or an escaped Shamu with the muscle tone to jump up and onto Highway A1A. But as the miles slowly ticked away with the setting sun, my death grip relaxed and even I had to admit there were worse places to die.

Since its beginning, Key West has been "out there." Ponce de León showed up in 1521 looking for the Fountain of Youth, evidently in vain, as he died later that year. When the island became a Spanish colony, fishing and salvage provided for the indigenous people.

Like a favorite Flea Market waaaaaay out of your neighborhood, Cayo Heuso as the island was called, became a popular trading port between Florida and Cuba. Over the years as control of the six-square-mile chunk of paradise bounced between Spain, Cuba, and Great Britain, its strategic importance grew due to its deep harbor, and location on the Straits of Florida. In 1822 Matthew C. Perry (no relation to Chandler Bing) planted the U.S. flag on "Thompson's Island." The island remained isolated from the mainland until 1912 when the Overseas Railway connected Key West to Florida. A hurricane in 1935 destroyed the railway, but by 1938 it had been rebuilt as a roadway to reach the southernmost point on the mainland. And in the twenty-first century, more than five hundred years after it was first populated, it still can take fourteen hours to travel from California to this westernmost key.

Key West's primary charm is, and probably always has been, its location. You don't end up in there by accident. And once you arrive, all you want to do is sit on the beach and have a few drinks. Thankfully, the locals are more than happy to oblige at authentic hangs like Captain Tony's, Sloppy Joe's, and the Green Parrot. Tourism is their lifeblood, and the city revels in catering to hardy adventurers like us who've trekked all this way to sleep only ninety miles from Cuba.

Of all the fantastically sublime places on the Key, Sunset Celebration at Mallory Square is the one not to miss. The daily ritual, complete with performance artists, driftwood artists, and con artists, is Key West distilled into one colorful, musical hour. "Sunset" has been the place to party since the 1960s, when local hippies started gathering every evening at the water's edge to watch as the sun extinguished itself in the warm waters of the Gulf, surrounded by pink and azure wisps. The bearded-seekers tripping on LSD saw the mythical Atlantis materialize in the clouds; people with jobs just saw bunnies, Elvis, and . . . clouds.

That free spirit remains today. No urban sprawl, no hectic traffic, just gorgeous tropical scenes, punctuated by bohemian artists and rum bars. Back in the day, Cuban cigars were big; nowadays smokes of all kinds lend their haze to the town's vibe. I think even the dogs are different. I threw a ball for a sheepdog, but he just waved his paw back and forth in front of his eyes and sighed. Does Key West change mainlanders into chillsters, or do low-Key transplants chill the island? It's a chicken and the egg paradox . . . which brings us to Key West's claim to fame: the Pie.

Back at the turn of the twentieth century, there were plenty of full-time residents of Key West. The island had plenty of fruit trees and many chickens . . . and therefore, eggs. But beef and milk were scarce because there were few, if any, cattle on the island. Cows were too smart to risk their lives on the bridges. Much like other Caribbean cultures, fish and chicken were the staples, with delicious fresh fruit for dessert. Food was made fresh every day, because there was no electricity and no refrigeration. It was a frontier life . . . which meant clever people were required.

Gail Borden was clever, but he didn't live in Key West. The condensed milk he invented in 1856 found its way down there because the cans could be easily packed into the hulls of ships and transported without temperature and time constraints. This versatility made this sweet milk in a can an indispensable part of the local diet. The new concoction was put to good use by Aunt Sally, the cook for Florida's first self-made millionaire, known in Key West as Rich Bill Curry. Sally is credited with creating the first Key lime pie.

Like any clever person, Sally used the ingredients she had—eggs, tart yellow Key limes, and Borden's condensed milk. The acid in the lime juice "cooked" the eggs, so all Sally had to do was whip all the ingredients together and pour it into a crust.

Simple? Wrong. Ever since, debate has raged over what, exactly, constitutes an authentic Key lime pie: cooked or uncooked, graham cracker or pastry crust, meringue or whipped cream on top. The only thing locals do agree on is color. Authentic Key lime pie is yellow, like the juice, not green like the food coloring added by char-latans seeking to fool unknowing mainlanders. A hurricane in 1926 wiped out most of the real Key lime trees and growers replaced them with Persian lime trees, which are easier to pick and ship. Since then, the few remaining authentic Key limes never leave Florida.

We began with the basics, a pilgrimage to the reigning goddess of pie,

COURTESY OF HENRIETTA'S ART OF BAKING/HENRIETTA

My FAVORITE . . . AIRLINE
Southwest

First of all, let's be real. In the past five years ALL AIRLINES have suffered a tremendous reduction in customer service and comfort. Due to economic problems, cutbacks, and union issues, the skies just aren't as friendly as they once were.

That being said, SOUTHWEST still gives you the biggest bang for your buck.

Let's start with the gate. Used to be, you had to hurry down to the gate two hours before departure and squat your position in line like a feral lemur to even hope to get a decent seat on the flight. But Southwest's new online check-in fixes that problem nicely.

You can check in up to twenty-four hours in advance. Which means, no matter where you are or what you're doing the day before, you can dial in on a smartphone or computer and check in. It takes about sixty seconds and gets you a virtual boarding pass with an A, B, C, or D on it. It will also have a number from 1 to 30. This "virtual line" means you can get to the gate at a reasonable time and wander until boarding. It also punishes people who aren't seasoned travelers, which always entertains me.

Since you checked in early, you are one of the first people on the plane, which means you get to pick a choice location. Sit near the front of the aircraft: more on that later. Exit rows are great if you've got long legs, and aisles are also a good idea. By the time the Cs and Ds make it into the aisle, there are only a few seats left, usually middle seats, almost always next to me. Now the turmoil begins.

I DO NOT like people sitting next to me in flight. I like room to stretch out and airplane seats are packed too tight. And though I love small talk on a barstool, at thirty thousand feet it drives me crazy . . . because I can't walk away when things go sour. Therefore, the goal is to keep the middle seat next to me EMPTY.

I've devised a foolproof way of accomplishing that difficult feat. Unless every single seat is filled, the one empty one will be at my side. How?

Germs. I've learned to make my eyes water on command, and can mess my hair and furrow my brow to give the impression that I'm a walking time bomb of some kind of flu that will ruin your trip to wherever we're headed.

I'll give you a moment to cluck your disapproval and judge me.

Now here's how you can do it too:

NEVER MAKE EYE CONTACT. This implies people are welcome to sit next to you. And as we've learned, they are not.

As the salesmen say, "ABC"—Always Be Coughing. As potential seat mates slow down and hover near your spot, preparing to put their bag in the compartment above— knowing full well the contents may shift during flight—it's time for you to spring into action.

Sneezing, coughing, perhaps seeing visions of deceased relatives . . . whatever you feel comfortable with is what you're after. Even if you do too much histrionics, it works. They might not believe you're sick, but they will know you're crazy. Just keep them moving down the line so they can ruin someone else's flight. Since you're sitting at the front of the plane, they won't feel the need to sit right away.

If you've screwed up by sitting near the back of the plane, sometimes even an Oscar-worthy performance won't work. They've walked long enough and will sit down, figuring you'll stop mini-barfing once the plane takes off.

Now, rather than ignore them, you become their best friend. Because you're smart, you didn't brush your teeth this morning, so the first thing you do to your new seatmate is say "HHHHHHHelllo," making sure to push up from the diaphragm. If the smell doesn't make them blink, you've still got work to do.

Turn to them mid-sniffle and start talking about your "illness."

"HHHHHHHHi, I'm Mark. Where're you headed today?" Without waiting for an answer, keep talking.

"I'm going to [pick a big hospital in the city you're landing in] so they can try and figure out what I've got. [Cough, cough, sniffle.] The bad news is the doctors say they've never seen this before, it's so contagious. Every time they try to study it, the researchers get sick, but the good news is when they figure it out, they're gonna name it after me. . . ."

And that's how you get first class room at a budget price. Enjoy the peanuts.

Henrietta Weaver, the owner and resident baking artist at the Art of Baking near the heart of Key West. Henrietta works with her son turning out creative Key lime treats, but she has become famous for her traditional Key lime pie. Together, we poured the sweet pudding into a graham cracker crust, topped it with meringue, and baked.

The resulting pie was tremendous: cool, refreshing, and tart. No wonder people down here in this muggy paradise loved these pies. It was like putting an air conditioner in your mouth. Henrietta's secret is in the juice. She doesn't use just Key lime juice; she uses a mix of several kinds of bottled lime juices to give her pies the perfect tart snap.

A short walk through Old Town reveals that these savvy shop-owners know which side of the bed their pie is buttered on. Every shop on the strand features something Key lime: cookies, fudge, chocolate sea shells, jelly beans, hard candy, soft candy, candy of indeterminate tensile strength, taffy, salsa, chutney, barbecue sauce, even salad dressing and tequila. And every shop has their take on Key lime pie.

> **No wonder people down here in this muggy paradise loved these pies. It was like putting an air conditioner in your mouth.**

Key West is charming. It's survived five hundred years of conquests, pirates, hurricanes, even Florida's Republican majority, and emerged stronger at every turn. And that's enough to draw people from all over the world to wander its streets and indulge in Key West's bohemian brand of Caribbean chic.

We did just that, then ended the day at Kermit's Key Lime shop with some Key lime margaritas. Kermit is the Wizard of

Odd. This spritely elf spends hours a day, frozen outside of his store, holding a pie like he's one of those realistic statues. When kids come up to him, he jumps and they scream. Screaming kids AND pie? I couldn't stay away. His kitschy corner is a one-stop shop for all things Key. And his margs don't skimp on the hooch.

Evening was approaching, so like everyone else in town, we gravitated to Mallory Square to see the show. The broad expanse of the square slowly begins to fill with revelers about ninety minutes before sundown. Most are curious tourists, but some are clearly regular members of the Key sun cult. They arrive with drinks in hand, colorful hats, and wide grins. Local artists set up booths to sell kites, incense, and tobacco water pipes (wink). Jugglers toss rings back and forth over the heads of startled grandparents as the sun slowly drops toward the pink clouds.

In this twilight, the bright colors of Key West's rainbow give way to the dark blue of the water and reveal the city's true nature. In the moments before night, I finally understood why locals and travelers alike gravitate to this open patch of land on the west side of the island. They come to enjoy . . . the island.

In minutes all of Key West appears, filling the square like they had been summoned by a silent gong to witness the certainty of the universe. With nothing but water stretching out forever toward the sun, Mallory Square becomes an astral observatory, showing anyone who's interested that, yes, there are still places to explore . . . somewhere over there.

Scattered individuals coalesce into a tribe, ohhing and ahhing in unison with every new color the clouds splay across the gray sky. Caribbean steel drums throb beneath laughter, while spicy, lime-drizzled grills sizzle in syncopation. Kids chase each other around seniors in their folding chairs, and for twenty minutes, no one has anyplace else they'd rather be.

THAT is Key West.

It's not the pie, the fishing, or the forty-two deathtrap bridges between Florida and its out-there outpost, it's that moment when you realize that, regardless of what it took to arrive, being here, now, gathered in circles around our big fireball, telling stories while darkness drapes the carnival, is enough.

Once the light is really, truly gone, applause fills the darkness. After the appreciation dies down, torches whoosh to life, casting a mamba-glow over the hunkered faces of travelers.

So just like humanity's first adventures, mine begins—hunkered around an ancient fire, listening to stories of far away.

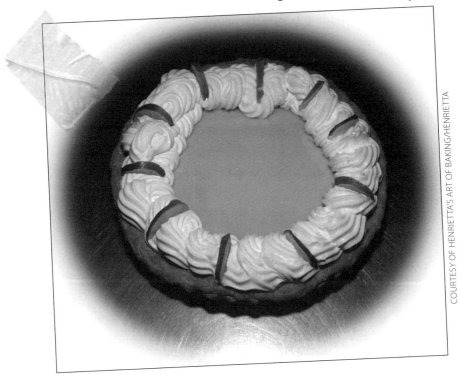

COURTESY OF HENRIETTA'S ART OF BAKING/HENRIETTA

HENRIETTA WEAVER'S ORIGINAL KEY WEST KEY LIME PIE

3 large eggs (separated)

1 can sweetened condensed milk

¼ cup Nellie & Joe's Key Lime Juice

¼ cup of Real Lime Juice

One 9-inch pie shell (baked)

¼ cup sugar

For the custard:

1. In medium bowl add three egg yolks slightly beaten.
2. Add condensed milk, mix well.
3. Slowly add lime juices, mix well. Custard will become thick. Pour custard into baked pie shell.
4. Bake at 325°F for 15 minutes.

For the meringue:

1. In large bowl, beat egg whites for 1 minute.
2. Add ¼ cup sugar, beat until it peaks.
3. Spread over baked pie.
4. Place pie back in oven for 8 to 10 minutes or until meringue is golden brown.
5. Place pie in refrigerator for 8 hours or overnight.

Eat it up!

Chapter 3
The Avocado's Name Is Kevin

The roadside terrain along US 101 morphs quickly from auto body shops to farmland once you're north of the smoggy Los Angeles basin. In no time, the crowded malls and endless traffic snarls transform into spacious outlet malls and fleeting traffic tiffs. And just beyond all of it, rows of green crops cover the rolling hills from the ocean to the mountains. Some are soybeans, some are veggies, and a lot are fruit trees—but not the ones you think. Up here, it's an avocado world . . . we just munch in it.

Santa Barbara County is the third largest avocado producer in North America. The soil, climate, and topography make it ideal for growing this versatile South American fruit, which in various varieties, has been around at least nine thousand years.

The avocado most of us eat today is the Hass, patented in 1935 in La Habra Heights, California. By the 1970s this varietal became America's leading avocado and now makes up about 90 percent of our crop. These warty, froggy pods grow from San Luis Obispo to Mexico and turn a gooey brown when left exposed to sunlight for more than ten minutes . . . just like Joan Rivers. But in the right hands, avocados transform into a condiment that is delicious to both eat and pronounce.

Avocados have long been popular in the Southwest, while somewhat of a mystery in the rest of the country due to their regional growing patterns. I grew up 1,700 miles from the fresh zone, so as a result, our Mexican food was crap. I am sure there were some places in downtown Chicago with good Mexican grub, but not any place a suburban kid like me could get to on his bike. Our real Mexican food was Taco Bell, because the only real Mexicans we knew, Pedro and Ron, worked there.

My two younger brothers and I would ride our bikes all the way past the stoplight on Ogden Avenue to visit them. I'd lead the parade on my Huffy, with Mike on his banana-seat Schwinn, and little Dan scurrying behind on his Big Wheel, and we'd go through the drive-thru to get our tacos. Not because they were so yummy, but because Pedro and Ron gave us unlimited salsa. The object of this ritual was to pile chunky salsa as high as possible above the taco top without spilling, then to eat it before wearing it.

For the uninitiated, the wet crunch of an over-salsa'd taco shell colliding with your younger brother's face is the funniest sound on earth. Honorable mention goes to the agonized "Oooof!" any guy, anywhere, makes when getting hit in the pills.

Perhaps because it was so mysterious, Mexican food was always a big deal at our house. Whenever Mom felt like raising the bar for a night, she'd announce "Mexican Night!" Tragically, this did not mean dressing us up as luchadors and scheduling bouts for our supper, winner take all. That would've been cool. Instead, she'd just brown some beef, toss in a packet of McCormick's seasoning, and lay out soft, flour tortillas on a plate. We'd overstuff them too, but the smush of soft tortilla on face isn't nearly as funny as crunchy tortilla—especially within Mom-retaliation range.

Unlike Taco Bell, Mom limited our salsa usage, but threw in a bonus: a mysterious, Kermit-colored tub of shiny goo, cryptically labeled "Zesty Guacamole-flavored Dip."

That was my guacamole: green sour cream from our grocer's dairy case. It wasn't real guacamole, but what did we know? Pedro and Ron never called it to our attention and it had the word guacamole printed right on the tub. How was I supposed to know that this flavored dip was as "ethnic"

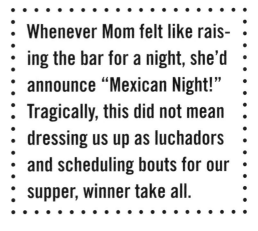

Whenever Mom felt like raising the bar for a night, she'd announce "Mexican Night!" Tragically, this did not mean dressing us up as luchadors and scheduling bouts for our supper, winner take all.

as truck stop pizza or Vanilla Ice? I just knew it tasted like next-day nacho cheese.

For years, I assumed all guacamole looked and tasted as bad as that jiggly, green goo, and I always made sure to avoid it. It wasn't until years later that I learned the truth.

I had moved to Southern California to attend UCLA. One night at work, I met a cute girl who wanted to take me to her favorite local place, an old Mexican joint in Koreatown, because she "loved their margaritas . . . and tequila makes me crazy!"

I borrowed my roommate's blue Buick LeSabre and zigged across town in record time, dodging throngs of seemingly driverless minivans while mentally preparing myself to endure a night of rotten Mexican food . . . all to savor a delicious Julie dessert.

El Cholo has been on the same rundown Los Angeles block since 1927, which qualifies the converted bungalow as Los Angeles's Great Pyramid. The adobe pueblo exterior, huge wooden door, and gang tags sprayed all over the parking lot didn't look like any Taco Bell I'd ever been to . . . except for the tagging. The savory smell of sizzling fajitas hung in the air like old lady perfume in a Denny's lobby. They called the bar a "cantina" and all the waitresses wore poofy, multicolored dresses that looked like layered drink umbrellas—more than authentic enough for me.

The cantina was packed, but parted willingly as Julie strutted, like only twenty-five-year-old dance majors can, up to the hostess, slipping her five bucks to seat us. I was twenty-two, and Julie was paying—Randy Newman was right, I LOVE L.A.

They sat us in back at a quiet table, Julie ordered a pitcher of Margs . . . and guacamole. As the waiter approached, I smiled and prepared to begin my gastronomic charade.

He looked like Zorro—to me at least—and dropped a big, black volcanic bowl in the middle of the table. Without speaking, he kneaded peeled avocados, onions, salsa, cilantro, and spices together like a master masseuse and topped it off with a squeeze of lemon. Then he slid the bowl across the polished table with a smirk and a shout, knowing he was delivering an epiphany.

"Guacamole!" Then, with a snap of his apron, he was gone.

THIS was guacamole? Not possible. It looked like a snot smoothie. But it couldn't be real snot because guys all over the dining room were eating it without getting yelled at by their dates. I looked across the goo-filled bowl at Julie. She smiled, dragged her finger through it, then slowly licked it clean.

"Ohhhh. Try it, you'll love it."

I was 51 percent sure she was talking about the guacamole, so I reached out and grabbed a chip . . . then froze. My brain said scoop, my stomach said run. A quick poll of other organs broke the tie.

I scooped a small glob and gave the guac a smell test. It reeked of authenticity . . . cilantro, peppers, and garlic, the gastronomic equivalent of Desi Arnaz belting out "Babalu" in my shower. (Yes, Desi was Cuban. But Robert Rodriguez singing James Taylor's "Mexico" in the foyer isn't as funny.)

This green stuff looked nothing like the flavored dip from my grocer's dairy case. It wasn't smooth— chunks of onion and tomato were lumped throughout the thick, salty paste. I slammed my fist down on the table—unlike the flavored dip, it didn't vibrate. The deep green color looked natural, not like it was made by radioactive Smurfs.

Julie slid closer and put her hand on mine, "Just try it . . . you won't be sorry."

She put my other hand onto her thigh. I scooped and ate. It could have been bison dung and toenail clippings and I would have still made yummy sounds. But after the roar in my ears subsided, I realized that she was right. Real guacamole is . . . really good. And I was in love.

Guacamole was the perfect complement to the hot, salty chip. She had spice, but wasn't hot. Her creamy pulp and juicy tomatoes tasted good on my tongue, and even better slathered all over my burrito. The bowl was scraped clean before the first margarita arrived. Guacamole's tangy, tart flavor had beguiled me on the first date. We'd definitely see each other again.

El Cholo is where I learned that a good guacamole is a great thing . . . almost as great as tequila. Over time, I also learned that guacamole recipes are like fingerprints. No two are the same, and some are criminal. Regardless, they are always a good predictor of a restaurant's overall deliciousness. A good guac won't guarantee you a great entrée, but when you get a crappy one, vamoose before the Manwich and processed American cheese arrive . . . even if you're dining with a "Julie."

Another hallmark of authentic Mexican food is the part we take for granted: the chip. You might think that tortilla chips came ashore from the belly of conquistador ships, or that the Mayans used them to scoop out still-beating hearts to make dramatic, and kinetic, snack trays, or that Zapata used overflowing bowls of "Yucatan Gold" to recruit the fiercest fighters in all of Mexico . . . but you'd be wrong.

The tortilla chip, ubiquitous yeoman of the fifth food group, and yin to the guacamole's yang, was invented at the El Zarape tortilla factory in Los Angeles, where corn and flour tortillas were made by hand for restaurants all over town.

It all started when El Zarape became one of the first companies to mass-produce tortillas by machine in 1947. At first, many of the tortillas got mangled by the machine, emerging misshapen or bent, and were thrown away. Then for a family party, Rebecca Webb Carranza, El Zarape's president, took some of the "defective" dough and "repurposed" it by deep-frying the resulting pieces. The chips were a hit at the party, even after Rebecca told her family they were basically fried refuse, and were soon selling for 10 cents a bag. By the 1960s, El Zarape's "Tort Chips" became their entire business.

Hass avocados haven't been around much longer. In less than eighty years, they've become sleepy Santa Barbara County's favorite kind of green. But popularity like this doesn't just happen. As American tastes became more international, growers realized they needed to find ways to promote their fruit outside of California. They tried everything they could think of to increase the demand. Rather than push the avocado as a stand-alone, like apples and oranges, they hitched their fortunes to my favorite condiment.

Actual archived industry newsletters are filled with a variety of "official" guacamole promotions, all propagated to ingeniously spike restaurant sales:

Guaco-Wacko Wing Dings—Guac with wings for dipping.
Avo-taco-saurus—Avo chunks in center spine of taco, slices
    for tail. Promote directly to children.
Play Guac 'n' Roll music—No explanation given.

Though exact tracking figures for these groundbreaking brain-bombs were too time-consuming for me to actually look up, the growers do say, in print, "more avocado penetration is needed." That's probably why in 1986, county leaders founded the California Avocado Festival as a way to celebrate the many delicious uses of the avocado . . . and grow more green.

America gets bashed for a variety of things. When it comes to fanny packs and sandals with socks, I agree. But there are some things we do right. At the very top of that list is festivals. There's something uniquely American about lining downtown with food booths, street dancing to '80s rock, and cheaply printed event t-shirts. I haven't read the Constitution in a while, but doesn't the Twenty-first Amendment basically require festivals?

The Romans and Greeks established festivals throughout the year to commemorate sacred cultural priorities. Today in America, we continue this hallowed tradition with festivals like Viola, Minnesota's Gopher Count Festival—where every June, folks turn in severed front gopher paws for $1.25 a pair; Whiting, Indiana's Pierogi Fest; and Pasadena's American Fancy Rat and Mouse Show.

Luckily, we didn't see any rats, fancy or otherwise, at the California Avocado Festival on the streets of downtown Carpinteria.

All we saw were avocados dressed up a la Mr. Potato Head, award-winning guacamole recipes, and the occasional cheerleader flying overhead.

Each year the Carpinteria High School cheerleaders mix up five thousand pounds of guacamole. In between pouring and stirring, they fling each other into the air to draw attention to their booth. Evidently, neither a kiddie pool filled with dip nor the initials "C.H.S." spelled out in salsa is enough to entice the passing throngs of jaded Guacamophiles to stop in and buy some tasty, green spirit!

Each booth along main street hawks a different avocado-flavored something: ice cream, soup, tortillas, salsa . . . as long as it was green, it sold. Many of the festers were the avocado farmers themselves, seemingly tickled that their ugly fruits could be transformed into such lovely delights.

The streets were choked with contests, live music, cooking demos, and of course what every festival needs . . . a mascot.

If you've ever been to Disneyland, or a minor league baseball game, you already know the mascot's Prime Directive: Thou Shalt Not Speak. Their other directives include: "Thou shalt not hug too hard," "Thou shalt not drink bourbon through your neck hole," and "Thou shall be able to take a punch from snotty kids while their parents aren't looking."

As one mascot wrangler told me, "Mascots are all about the illusion for the kids. If they speak, it's ruined."

Does that mean if they don't, kids believe there's an actual avocado dancing down the street to a crappy version of "Johnny B. Goode?" That's not good. How many times have you seen kids screaming in terror as giant "whatevers" walk up to them and gesture wildly? Toddlers don't understand that the giant box of popcorn isn't real. All they know is that it's way bigger than it should be and it's chasing them. Those are the kinds of extreme experiences that scar kids for life. Years later, these kids morph into teenagers who break into a cold sweat every time they see a tub of popcorn at the movies. It's been a while since I've taken a high school girl to the movies, but I'm pretty sure breakdowns like that would be discussed in the lunchroom. Loudly.

> **Toddlers don't understand that the giant box of popcorn isn't real. All they know is that it's way bigger than it should be and it's chasing them.**

That's why whenever I see a mascot, I always try to engage them in conversation. It's my crusade. I start with simple yes and no questions to draw them in. Then, once I have their rapt attention, I badger them with questions I know they're dying to answer . . . but require complete sentences.

And I'm not just talking out of my plush. Back when I was at UCLA, I was a mascot. In fact, that's how I met Julie.

The California Lottery had just announced a new game that featured the four suits in a deck of cards. They hired four people, two guys to play "Spade" and "Club," and two women to play "Diamond" and "Heart." I was "Spade" and Julie was "Heart."

They paid me $1,000 a day to go around to sporting events and malls, dressed in black tights with my face sticking out of a giant Ace of Spades card. They told us to be silent, but I just couldn't. Standing around dressed as a playing card was embarrassing . . . unless I was talking smack. It caught people off-guard. No one really knew what to say to a giant card in dance tights, which just made me talk to them more.

I especially enjoyed walking up to sexy mommies and asking if they preferred diamonds or spades. Mostly, they'd just stare and stammer . . . until their husbands pulled them away.

And though it's been years, I still feel part of that unique plush brotherhood. By talking to the mascots, I guess I'm trying to set them free. Sadly it never worked . . . until I met Kevin.

I was sitting on the curb, munching on some avocado salsa when I saw him: six feet tall, green and silly, walking out from behind a fence. Mr. Avocado strutted down the street like he owned the place.

Usually mascots travel with a handler, but not Mr. Avocado. He was perfectly comfortable squishing around on his own. I gave Mr. A. a half-hearted "How's it going, Greenie," knowing all I'd get in return is some mimed response.

"Good."

It talked? I spoke again.

"Great day for a festival, huh?"

"Yep."

It was no dream. He'd stopped walking and was just standing there. I was having a real conversation with a fake avocado. My heart started beating faster. "So . . . What's your name?"

Mascots always had funny names. From Speedy Alka-Seltzer to McGruff, a mascot's nothing without a catchy handle.

"Kevin."

"Kevin?"

"Yeah."

"What kind of avocado are you?"

"Green."

"No, I mean what varietal?" Brian slid quietly off to the side and gave me the thumbs up. I began preparing my Emmy acceptance speech.

"Green, I think."

He was being evasive, perhaps sensing the camera. Time to go for the gold.

"So what's your favorite Mexican place up here? Where do you stand on the slaughter of your innocent brothers and sisters for the sake of a delicious appetizer? Is it hard to find pants that don't make you look fat and lumpy?"

As he started to answer, I heard a commotion behind me, but like Mike Wallace, I kept the mic in his face and barked more incisive questions.

"Do you have any super powers?"

But before Kevin could answer, a screaming teenage guy in a t-shirt and green tights leapt over a line of trash cans and grabbed Kevin by the shoulders, shaking him so violently his sunglasses flew off.

"Stop the filming. Stop it right now! This is an imposter!" The teenager scrambled to the glasses, and gingerly replaced them on Kevin's bulbous green head/body as if they were Vatican relics. He stepped back and pointed an accusing finger at Kevin with all the subtlety of a bad high school production of *The Crucible.*

"He isn't the real Mr. Avocado. I AM the REAL MR. AVOCADO!! Look. LOOK AT MY LEGS!"

With that he stuck his spindly, green legs toward the camera and did an elfish shuffle step. Festival officials arrived on the scene, and a guy wearing an "Event Security" windbreaker barked into his walkie.

"Base, we've got a 10-34, 10-34 at the Dumpsters!"

There was an existing 10-code for fruit-jacking? As radios all over the street crackled to life, we became the center of a full-fledged incident. Three more Event Security sheepishly detained the giant avocado while I tried to pry him free. This was the kind of hijinks that can come back to prevent a Senate candidacy down the road. I didn't want that for Kevin.

"Of course he's Mr. Avocado," I pleaded. "Look at him."

"Yes, LOOK AT HIM," Greenie screamed. "He's wearing jeans. Mr. Avocado always wears green tights. Ask anyone."

Ask anyone? In that instant, I knew Kevin was an imposter. Not because of the jeans. But because Greenie was so ridiculously fixated on the mythology of Mr. Avocado that he assumed that everyone in the English-speaking world would be intimately familiar with his official wardrobe. Only the real Mr. Avocado could be that much of a doofus.

On screen, you see what happens next. Greenie rips the suit off the avocado's body, revealing a skinny teenager . . . named Kevin. Then Greenie starts reciting his resume directly to camera.

"I've played Mr. Avocado for EIGHT YEARS. I've been in all the commercials. I'm in the print ads. I was the model for the poster. This kid is an imposter!"

A uniformed sheriff that Greenie flagged down asks Kevin if this is true. He slumps and mumbles, "Yes."

"How do we know you're not an imposter too?" I ask Greenie. "Let's see you fit into that thing."

Greenie turns to me, filled with as much righteous indignation as a skinny twerp in green tights carrying a giant avocado head can command, and declares, "No. Not here. Not where the children can see."

And with that, Greenie dashed like Superman into a nearby phone booth . . . except it was a Porta-Potty.

Greenie vanishes, but he can't quite fit the costume inside behind him, creating the delicious moment when three sheriffs, five Event Security off-duty sheriffs, a TV crew, and a detained Kevin stare in snarky disbelief as

> **He can't quite fit the costume inside behind him, creating the delicious moment when three sheriffs, five Event Security off-duty sheriffs, a TV crew, and a detained Kevin stare in snarky disbelief as a giant avocado struggles to squeeze itself inside a large plastic pooper.**

a giant avocado struggles to squeeze itself inside a large plastic pooper. Savor the visual . . .

By the time Greenie finally managed to pull the door shut behind him, there was a gapers' block of youngsters three rows deep circling the crapper, listening with rapt attention to the thumps and bumps echoing from inside. It'd taken decades, but I finally heard a sound funnier than tacos smushing into my brother's face.

While Greenie rocked the potty back and forth, the sheriff got Kevin's story. He was just some kid at the fest with his friends when they saw the suit lying on the ground near the bushes during Greenie's break. They all dared each other to grab Mr. Avocado, but only Kevin had the schnardines to pick it up, put it on, and become Mr. Avocado.

He didn't steal it. He didn't deface it. He just wore it and walked through the crowd, feeling the love. What a thrill it must have been—the adoring looks of avocado fans, the smiles of children, the thoughtful questions of the TV host. Such a thrill, in fact, that he broke the #1 rule of teen pranks . . . and gave his real name.

Remember kids, whenever you're out and up to no good, never, ever, NEVER use your own name when apprehended. For best results, always have a good fake name in mind before the hijinks ensue. That way you're not forced to come up with one under duress.

After a few minutes, the jostling inside the Porta-Potty calmed, the door flew open, and out squeezed Mr. Avocado! He smoothed his tights and strode gloriously into the limelight.

Standing at my side, a perplexed seven-year-old stared at the toilet in disbelief, his head cocked like a Labrador. I leaned down and looked him dead in the eye.

"Everybody poops, kid."

Mr. Avocado danced across the lawn. He pranced for the camera. He hugged (appropriately) every child that ran up to him: all without ever uttering a sound.

During the kiddie love-rush, Kevin slipped away. The sheriff didn't seem to care, but Mr. Avocado was irate. I think. His hands were on his hips. He pointed emphatically as Kevin slipped into the crowd, and he wagged his finger in the sheriff's face. He seemed irate-ish, but I wasn't convinced. I mean, anyone who was really irate . . . would SAY something!

Finally, the real Mr. Avocado took his cue. He stood in front of the camera, miming all the classics—making "yummy circles" on his stomach at people eating guacamole, pretending to mix up a batch of guacamole, and . . . dancing.

He was dying to be interviewed. But I just couldn't; it felt like a betrayal of Kevin, so I just kept asking him questions that couldn't be answered with yes or no questions. I think it made him even more irate. At least I hope it did.

After a few moments of hands-on-hips attitude, Mr. Avocado stalked off into the crowd, and just like that, the great security breach was over. The threat level was lowered back to "Green" and the festival continued as if nothing had happened.

We spent the rest of the day surfing the festival, eating fresh produce, and enjoying the sunshine. We talked to farmers, students, parents, and their kids. Everyone was just happy to be there, and couldn't wait to tell us, on camera, how delicious avocados were. We felt like neighbors.

In towns small enough where people actually know and talk to each other, a festival is more block party than sales event. Everyone shows up to sell their wares, but it's really just an

My Favorite . . . NIGHTLIFE

In WINTER: Las Vegas

It's warm enough to walk around without slushing through snow and sleet. There's always a great concert, headliner, or show within earshot and some of the casinos stay open past 9:00 p.m.

Whether you're looking for clubs, dancing, music, that exhibit where they peel the skin off real people and show how the body works, Vegas has it in spades. Check the Web sites ahead of time, and call hotels to get VIP rates and free tickets to stuff. There are constantly changing deals on rooms and food, but one thing is always the same: If you pay retail, advertised price, you paid too much, rube.

In SPRING: New York

Shaking the layers of coats and fat off its communal body, the Big Apple comes out of hibernation in the spring. Baseball, hockey, and basketball rage across the island virtually every night, while clubs, restaurants, and concerts pump music through the newly reopened windows. As more outdoor activities come back on line, Broadway shows become easier to book but restaurant space gets tighter.

In SUMMER: Chicago

You want to get there before August, when the humidity index approaches Stephen Hawking's IQ.

The explosion of color, activities, and people who've spent the winter and frigid spring locked inside their cubicles is like a Big Bang of fun. Check out the www.CityofChicago.org to see a complete list of city festivals, music events, and neighborhood fests. Literally every weekend in Chicago, somebody's having a big throwdown with food, music, and people you want to hang out with. If you are bored during the summer in Chicago, slap the loser in your mirror.

In FALL: New Orleans

Bourbon Street never sleeps. Really.

Summer is too hot, and winter can be too wet, so fall wins by default. Like Chicago, NOLA is always throwing block parties, music fests, and food extravaganzas. Google "New Orleans Live Music" and enjoy 130 pages of mojo. Always talk to your hotel concierge to get steered in the right direction, unlike the grifters who do this job in some other cities, NOLA concierges respect the food and music of their city too much to steer you to anyplace they wouldn't go themselves. The Ritz, Roosevelt, Crowne Plaza, and Montelone usually house all the musicians in town, so they make it their business to find out who might be sitting in with whom, and where.

Halloween weekend is a great time to go because that's when the Voodoo Experience takes over City Park. Part Jazz Fest, part Burning Man, the Voodoo Experience rages deep into the night with some of the best music acts rocking today. Nighttime in NOLA never felt so good.

excuse to hang out for the day. Chefs walk the streets passing out treats, kids chase other kids, and people call out the names of schoolmates . . . from thirty years ago. It's like a Capra movie, only in color.

> Chefs walk the streets passing out treats, kids chase other kids, and people call out the names of schoolmates . . . from thirty years ago. It's like a Capra movie, only in color.

In L.A., you can't walk six steps at a street festival without literally bumping into a BlackBerry zombie or some breathless goon gushing about their screenplay . . . to some disinterested sidekick playing with their iPhone. Everybody talks, nobody listens, and commerce trumps camaraderie.

But not at the Avocado Festival. I spent over an hour in the tent with the cheerleaders, helping them mix their five thousand pounds of guac. These little girls were using a kayak oar to stir it all up. It looked strenuous, so I volunteered to help. It was like mixing cement. I don't know how they did it all day, unless I was just the most recent stooge to help them whitewash their fence. All we talked about was boys, cheers, and giggling. I also learned, for all time, how to spell "guacamole" out loud.

I felt like I was back in school myself, spending all night working on UCLA's Rose Parade float inside some dark hangar in Pasadena. Back when nobody got paid—unless you count cold beer and pizza, all we made were memories.

I stared into that 2.5 tons of guac and realized that being part of something—a town festival, a school float, the guy who

gathered the phone numbers of all the girls who thought they were just filling in contact information in case our float won, is really what festivals are about.

On our way out of town, our car passed Kevin and his friends sitting in an alley, laughing. Maybe that's what Kevin wanted— to be a part of something. Maybe he and his scruffy alley cats just wanted to join the rest of the town on their big day and play a part in the show. So, invited or not, they did. And, regardless of the reception, their smiles said it had been a good day.

Kevin waved, then turned back to continue the story he'll tell every September, whenever his lifelong buds get together on these streets to eat sweet treats, march in the sun, and watch the cheerleaders fly.

CARPINTERIA HIGH SCHOOL CHEERLEADERS GUACAMOLE

Feeds a Festival

Avocados (5,000)
Diced onions (100 pounds)
Diced tomatoes (50 pounds)
Lemon juice (2 gallons)
Salt (to taste)
Pepper (to taste)
Garlic (to taste)

COURTESY OF LAURIE CHAMLEE

Chapter 4
Fruitcake Monks

 It was 7:00 a.m. and the padre was pissed.

We had just arrived at a Godforsaken kitchen, sixty miles from Louisville, Fort Knox, or Bourbon County, to a less than Fatherly welcome.

"You're late," he barked. His ornate crucifix bounced in rhythm to his frail, thrusting arms.

I knew today was gonna be hell. We were scheduled to roast all day in a monastic bakery, churning out re-giftable chum for the holiday food chain—fruitcake. We'd been driving since before sunrise, so if anyone should've had his vestments in a twist, it was me, not the wrinkled, scowling surrogate of Christ blocking our entrance with his clipboard.

I don't do mornings. I've spent my entire career working nights . . . and I love it. I'm always better at 2:00 a.m. in a comedy or music club than I can ever be at a breakfast club. My best days on the *Taste of America* road were nights spent in the kinds of dive joints that sponsor both a softball and a bowling team, arguing and laughing with strangers. Waking up early for work really put a damper on that fun. So I didn't.

But for this one day, I had grudgingly agreed to get up early and start at sunrise . . . because, according to Queen d'Office Judy, "That's when the monks bake. And they want to show us everything. They're so sweet."

We'd made it to the 150-year-old Gethsemani Abbey in Trappist, Kentucky, before the sun, ready to shoot these supposedly cherubic monks mixing, whipping, and shoving goo and green cherries into fruitcake shape. According to our schedule, by starting at seven, we'd have just enough time to bake and wrap 'em before leaving for the airport. "We waited all morning! You were supposed to be here at SIX!" The geezer gestured to the five monks working hard behind him, "These fruitcakes can't wait!" I bit my lip and turned away . . . too easy.

"Our schedule reads seven . . . ," I explained.

"It's wrong." The monk folded his arms menacingly and blocked the door. We asked to see the person in charge. The old man squinted from under his cockeyed baseball cap. "You're looking at him. I'm Brother Raphael."

It all came rushing back at me like the maniacal ear twist at the end of a nun's fingers. This Raphael . . . he was one of "them": one of those tyrannical nuns and priests who left indelible marks on my body and psyche during twelve years of Catholic schooling.

Sure, in hindsight, I realize we were all just doing our jobs. They were trying to teach a class full of smartass suburban kids, and I was trying to squirt milk out the noses of said punks with various jokes, gags, and pranks. (Grades one through eight: My 623 nose squirts still stands as an Illinois record—modern era.) Over time, I forged a grudging respect with my teachers. All but one.

Sr. Margaret Jean ran her classroom like a cell block. A snarling, smelly fireplug of a woman, she exhibited unabashed delight in crushing any of her eighth grade male students—mentally and physically—that had the gall to exhibit joy or enthusiasm or to look directly into her brown beady eyes.

Her voice sounded like chalk on the devil's blackboard; her crooked teeth looked like she'd spent years chewing on a junkyard fence. For the record, she also had a mustache and smelled like old cheese.

I'm still not convinced that there is an actual hell, but I hope so. Satan will have something really evil lined up for Margaret Jean: maybe cleaning an infinite school hallway . . . with a toothbrush . . . while happy children dance circles around her bent, twisted body, tracking mud and splurting Bic ink in her wake. Yeah . . . that's some goooood hell.

So it was that the glowering snarl of Brother Raphael brought this vindictive shrew swirling back into my slowly waking mind.

"You're late." A Mexican standoff at a French monastery with a geriatric monk, all part of today's balanced breakfast.

We just stood there, looking at each other. Half awake, I was breathing deeply in an effort to end my smelly flashback. Out of options, I smiled and tossed up a Hail Mary.

"I'm sorry, we made a mistake. Can't we figure something out? You've got such a kind face."

In an instant, he was a totally new Bro.

Brother Raphael's face broke out into a huge smile, with sparkling eyes and soft features. He threw open the kitchen doors and unlocked his arms.

"Thank you. How can we help?" And that was that. Like he'd been playing an elaborate practical joke. Like it never happened.

We were escorted into a Wonka-like wonderland where monks, short and tall, fat and small, churned the batter, fired the ovens, and sprinkled fruits and pecans in perfect synchronicity.

Catholic monks have been quietly living, working, and praying at the abbey since it was founded by the French in 1848. Probably the most famous resident was author Thomas Merton, a Trappist at Gethsemani from 1941 until his accidental death in 1968, who championed silence, solitude, and prayer as the way to become one with God. Merton's autobiography, *The Seven Storey Mountain,* sold a million copies. That same lifestyle of quiet industry continues with the monks of today.

The days at the oldest and largest Trappist monastery in the Western world begin at 3:00 a.m., with a call to prayer. Then they bake, pray, eat, and repeat, until they sleep. Tomorrow, they wake up and do it all again. For half a century they've been supporting this lifestyle by selling monk-made specialty foods through the mail. Today, their wares include cheese, bourbon fruitcake, and bourbon fudge—it is Kentucky. God works in mysterious ways . . . and now at broadband speed.

COURTESY OF GETHSEMANI FARMS MONASTERY

For a *Taste of America* holiday special, we were collecting dishes for a holiday feast from all over, then throwing a big party at my Aunt Cookie's house in Chicago. As we researched other traditional Christmas recipes—turducken, cranberries, calamari—we realized we couldn't throw a holiday feast without a fruitcake.

But rather than a syrupy, gloppy mess, we set out to find the best fruitcake in America, one that was more than edible, a fruitcake that was . . . un-regiftable. All signs, and over one hundred thousand satisfied customers a year, pointed to Gethsemani.

> **Yep, like indoor toilets and funny-looking numerals, fruitcake started with the Romans.**

Who was the first guy to add fruit to cake? History isn't sure, but he probably had a vowel at the end of his name. Yep, like indoor toilets and funny-looking numerals, fruitcake started with the Romans.

Back in the days of the Empire, they used pomegranate seeds, pine nuts, and raisins mixed into barley mash, and preserved it with honey and spices to make their fruitcake. Chock full of dried fruits and nuts, the cake did not spoil quickly, and proved to be a nutritious food for armies—and other wandering Italians—in their travels through the Mediterranean and elsewhere.

The area between the Strait of Gibraltar and the Dead Sea was ripe with nuts and fruits, and over time, the ingredient list of fruitcake expanded to include most of these eclectic local treats.

Plentiful sugar from the colonies in the 1600s resulted in an excess of candied fruits, making fruitcakes more available and affordable. In Europe, these newly available fruits were exotic and delicious—especially given the bland diets of the day—and fruitcakes quickly gained in popularity at weddings and holidays.

During the 1700s, fruitcakes were baked at the end of each year's nut harvest, but kept until the following year before being consumed. This enlightened ritual was believed to ensure continued prosperity . . . much like burning a witch or not washing your hands before performing surgery.

In the days before refrigeration, food preservation was more important than taste. Meats weren't salted for better flavor, as anyone who's ever taken a beef jerky road trip knows. Rather, salting produces a high protein, very portable food with a virtually limitless shelf life. The alcohol content and dried ingredients in fruitcake created a rich food with a similarly extended lifespan. To my great surprise, history reports that there was a time when people were actually happy to receive a fruitcake. That was then. . . .

In twenty-first century America, weren't fruitcakes just a gift for Christmas gagging? Turns out, I had plenty to learn . . . and not just about fruitcake.

We spent the next eight hours with Brother Raphael. He showed us around the abbey, took the extra fruitcake batter he had secretly saved for us, and demonstrated the process of making the cakes with an easy smile. He proudly introduced all the other baking Brothers, and we taped the whole procedure, start to finish, and had everything we needed to create a great segment. We even had enough dough left over to bake delicious cookies. While they were baking, Brother Rae took us to lunch.

There are three places to eat in the Trappist monastery. We ate in the one dining room where talking was allowed. Because we had started work sooo early, we had everything shot but our final taste test, so we could just relax and talk until the cakes were done baking. It was the best business lunch of my life.

Brother Raphael Prendergast was born in St. Louis in 1922. He grew up in a house of fifteen, "a fun house" where someone was always playing a prank—like the cranky monk prank he'd played on us this morning. Growing up during the Depression with twelve brothers and sisters could have been horrible, but Brother Rae had a ball. Things were great until World War II broke out; that's when he enlisted in the Navy and ended up on an aircraft carrier.

"What is it like to be a chaplain on a carrier?" I asked him as we munched on surprisingly tasty pasta.

"I wasn't a chaplain. I was a fighter pilot. I flew Corsairs. Afterwards, I taught Navy pilots instrument flying in Pensacola for eight years. Instruments. The thing I hated most about flying . . . I was teaching it eight hours a day. I've only been here since 1954."

Only 1954.

After years of teaching young men how to fly and kill for their country he couldn't continue, and somehow found his way back to the Midwest. Perhaps drawn by the publicity of Merton and his writings, he officially became Brother Raphael in 1959.

Fighter pilot to silent baker?

"Though you wouldn't think so, there are a lot of commonalities between flying and faith. When you're up in that cockpit, flying through clouds or at night, using just your instruments . . . you need faith. Faith in your instruments and in your training. You might feel like the plane is flying level, really feel like it, but if your gauges say you're not, what do you believe? That belief is the difference between life and death."

"And here's another thing. When you're flying by radio, by radar, you triangulate your position by listening for the pings.

60

You're trying to find your way home, and your radio is listening for pings. Using two fixed points, you're able to zero in on your home tower . . . but the paradox is that when you finally get back home, the pings cancel out and it's totally quiet. When you're home, there is nothing. So you're looking for that nothingness. That stillness. Just being. That's God."

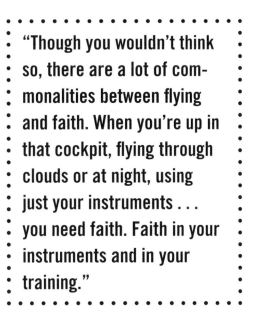

"Though you wouldn't think so, there are a lot of commonalities between flying and faith. When you're up in that cockpit, flying through clouds or at night, using just your instruments . . . you need faith. Faith in your instruments and in your training."

I attended twelve years of religion class and never heard anything remotely that profound. No bluster, no fire and/or brimstone. No guilt or mindless prohibitions. Just a trained killer-trainer dropping his Aero-Zen on me, then watching it blow my mind. Without missing a chomp, his tao of 1940s naval radar explained what years of pretending to read the Bible, and actually reading Stephen Hawking could not. THAT'S a teacher.

He talked about the biblical creation story and how it aligned with modern physics' Big Bang Theory. He acknowledged the mistakes of organized religion. He talked about "the noise" of our modern world. Rae believed that modern noise can drown out the inner voice belonging to . . . guess who.

We talked all afternoon, alternating between profound and profane insights into humanity and whatever it is that lies just beyond the reach of our intellect. Can't wrap your head around the pings and tower, no problem. Brother Rae will explain humanity's earthly spiritual quest using language you do know. He'll talk hardware to a plumber or music to a honky-tonk piano player. And if you've got a food show on the Travel Channel, he'll talk baseball.

Yeah, he played pro ball for a while too. Before the war, he paid the bills throwing heat in leagues around the Midwest. If it was anyone else, anywhere else, I'd assume it was all BS. But something about the outfit—and his grin—convinced me he'd simply led a fantastic life.

And now he was writing it all down, so that we can know the stuff he's dredged up during his eight decades of life surfing.

At eighty-four, he was the most full of life person I'd ever met, one of those people you can watch think. I'd say something; he'd pause and consider, then respond. I'll admit that at first it was strange to have someone actually listen to me, but I got over it.

Dusk was falling on my afternoon of enlightenment. We'd walked all the way around the monastery and it was time to go back and get the fruitcakes off the cooling shelf . . . and eat one.

TASTING TIME—the part of my day that always caused me the most angst. Typically by this point in our workday, I've spent hours with our guest; we've bonded and become pals. We've laughed together, we've cooked together, and now it's time to eat their most treasured treat. Not as easy as it sounds. I do a delicate dance when their "delicious" morsel is pulled out of the pot and/or oven and offered to me like manna from heaven.

Their expectant look always makes me smile. At that moment, what they're offering me, it's not food—it's a piece of

themselves—or their ancestors—or their livelihood, but always more than just food.

Luckily, most of the time it's good. Sometimes it's GREAT. And a few times . . . just awful. Total crap. But I decided long ago that I wasn't going to be one of those pandering hosts—you know who they are—who just love everything. What's the point of THAT?

It would also disrespect the chefs who make food that I really DO like. It's personal preference—not an indictment of the chef's entire family. Luckily most of our guests understand that . . . except the bug guy. But that's another chapter.

I call 'em as I taste 'em. So it was as the smiling Brother Rae pulled his fruitcakes off the cooling racks and offered me the first bite.

Disclaimer: I HATE fruitcake. We don't need it anymore to ward off scurvy or bring good luck to our harvest. We've got Archer Daniels Midland for that. As a society, we're over fruitcake, but on this episode, I had to pretend we're not.

It's squishy, too syrupy sweet, and the "fruit" in it is usually blue and too red. According to Wikipedia, fruitcakes are regifted 140 percent of the time. Do the math. Sadly, the monk's fruitcake didn't look any better.

But I was torn. By now, I was crazy about this geezer. This smiling, laughing poet who'd lived more lives than a cat wanted me to try his fifty-year-old recipe on

Disclaimer: I HATE fruitcake. We don't need it anymore to ward off scurvy or bring good luck to our harvest. We've got Archer Daniels Midland for that.

My Favorite . . . PIZZA

Pizano's on State Street, Chicago, Illinois

"Pizza?" is a loaded question in Chicago.

Thick or thin: Thick. What are you, a jagoff?

Ambience: Bring your own bowie knife to carve your name into the wall. Impresses the girls.

Beer or wine: South Siders chug Old Milwaukee Light, North Siders sip Shiraz.

Five stars or one: Do you want to wipe sauce and cheesy strings on linen napkins, or paper placemats printed with the "History of Pizza"?

First, if you've never been to Chicago before, hit Gino's East, Due's, or Uno's. Endure the lines, order the cheese and sausage, and drink Old Style for forty-five minutes waiting for The Rapture.

Giordano's stuffed pizza is great, for those times when a six-pound slice just isn't enough, and Lou Malnati's tangy sauce and cornmeal–free dough is not to be missed. But everybody knows those places.

My pick is a find, yet springs from this royal bloodline. The owner's father, Rudy Malnati Sr., basically invented deep dish pizza in 1943 when he opened Pizzeria Uno. Since then Chicago's pizza underworld has featured more intrigue and double-crossing than *Goodfellas*. Today, Rudy Jr. carries the rolling pin for original, Chicago deep dish pizza.

Pizano's looks like Louis in the Bronx (where Michael whacks Sollozzo and the police captain) and features a great neighborhood bar. Great place to catch a Cubs game or argue about why most Sox fans don't seem to have dental.

They're flexible at Pizano's. Wedding reception? Sure. Post-softball beer joint? Yep. Al fresco lunch that you can smell from Michigan Avenue three blocks away? Si. Take two deep dish (a "Rudy" and a "Hey Hey!"), and thank me in the morning.

COURTESY OF PIZANO'S/KEY MAGAZINE

national TV . . . and I was going to HATE it. What to do? I could tell him the truth: "No wonder no one talks in your dining hall . . . they're too busy choking on this crap."

Or to save his feelings, I could break my Golden Rule, and lie . . . to A MONK! That's GOT to be worse than lying to a civilian. I know the church: It's all about hierarchy and retribution.

THE MOMENT OF TRUTH had arrived. The camera was rolling as this cherub's thin, delicate hand held out my fruity destiny. Trash his pride & joy, not to mention livelihood, or look him straight in his pale blue eyes and lie my ass off? I took a bite.

COURTESY OF BRIAN MILLER

Hallelujah chorus! IT WAS DELICIOUS! Honestly. The key to this monky fruitcake was that it wasn't too sweet. It wasn't soaking in syrup like the 140 percent fruitcakes. Somehow the monks had figured a way to make it look like a fruitcake—very important for catalog sales to grandparents—while making it taste like a cookie/cake hybrid—very important for eating. The fruit tasted like real fruit. The cake was light, moist, but not soggy, and the nuts were crunchy. The whole thing reminded me of a buffed-up carrot cake with added sass. Swear to God.

I felt like I was tossing my crutches into the Dumpster at Lourdes. The monks did it! They made a fruitcake that was not only edible, but desirable. Will miracles never cease? As I gushed praise for his creation, Brother Rae just looked on and smiled. He knew it all along. Ping!

Relief! Between the four of us, the crew polished off the entire cake. That says it all. We'd become such food snobs working on the show, anything more than the courtesy bite was the ultimate praise.

The sun was setting as we packed for our long trip home. Before we left, I made Brother Raphael promise to send me a copy of his epic-in-progress. It's one good book I can't wait to read.

We hugged then drove away. No pings . . . just GPS.

Months went by, but I never heard from Brother Rae. The show aired, and everyone loved the segment. Not a word from the silent monk. He couldn't possibly be unhappy with the show . . . maybe this was another monk prank. After a few unanswered e-mails, I knew something wasn't right.

Finally, I got an e-mail through my Web site—not from the monks, but from a civilian who had spent some time on a retreat at the abbey years ago, and stayed in touch with Brother Raphael. He was one of the legions of friends Rae had made over his half-century at the abbey.

He had news. Raphael had passed away in June after a brief illness. He also told me the pitching/flying/teaching/laughing Brother had enjoyed our segment when it aired. He had continued working on his book until the end as well. I've asked the abbey to see the book, but it's too soon.

Perhaps one day they will offer it for sale along with their fruitcakes. It would be a fitting tribute to a man for many, many seasons. Drop them a line at www.monks.org and ask for your copy of the book.

PING!

FAT-FREE FRUITCAKE

The monks take their vow of silence very seriously; in fact they won't say a word about their fruitcake recipe, which is why there are so many crappy fruitcakes clogging up the Postal Service every holiday season.

However, I found a family recipe . . . and changed it to make a fat-free fruitcake.

Give it a shot . . . when you realize it's not as good as the Gethsemani Farms version . . . order theirs online and you'll get your "Ping!" too.

8 ounces nonfat cream cheese

¾ cup light brown sugar, packed

4 eggs

3 cups all-purpose flour

1 teaspoon baking soda

1 teaspoon salt

2 teaspoons cinnamon

1 cup molasses

½ cup milk

1½ cup mixed dried fruit, coarsely chopped (dried cranberries, dried cherries, dried blueberries)

1 cup chopped walnuts

1 tablespoon grated lemon rind

1 tablespoon grated orange rind

2 teaspoons vanilla

½ cup corn starch

CITRUS GLAZE

1.5 ounces Kentucky bourbon

Grapefruit juice

1 cup of powdered sugar

DAY ONE

1. Preheat oven to 325°F (165°C). Butter a 6x3 inch round pan, and line with parchment paper.
2. In a large metal bowl, cream together cream cheese and brown sugar until fluffy. Beat in eggs.
3. Whisk together flour, baking soda, salt, and cinnamon; mix into butter and sugar in three batches, alternating with molasses and milk.
4. Stir in the dried fruit and chopped nuts, lemon and orange rind, vanilla, and corn starch. Scrape batter into the prepared pan.
5. Bake for 40 to 45 minutes. Cool in the pan.

DAY TWO

1. Insert a 5-inch needle—or other appropriate tool—into the cake in three places, injecting about 1.5 ounces of Kentucky bourbon into the cake.
2. Mix grapefruit juice and powdered sugar into a spread using a whisk.
3. Spread Citrus Glaze on top of the cake, wrap in airtight container, and store for approximately six weeks before enjoying.

Chapter 5
Wings of Addiction

It was Labor Day and we were on the infield at Dunn Tire Park in Buffalo, New York, under a blazing sun. This day was all about crowning a new champion, a kiddie pool filled with blue cheese dressing, and America's most debilitating teenage addiction. Yep, today was about WINGS.

Not the Linda McCartney band. Not the mysteriously successful '80s sitcom. Not even the plastic ones you get on Southwest if you agree to stop heckling Nadine during her safety manifesto.

No, this Labor Day was all about buffalo wings. And by the power vested in me by basic cable, I'd get to spend this holiday working as a court jester to the Chicken King.

Personally, I can't endure an entire holiday weekend without satisfying my festival mojo. They're not hard to find if you know where to look. Pick a food, activity, sport, or hobby, and somewhere, someone in America is waiting right now, ready to sell you beer tickets and a t-shirt.

In Buffalo, that man is Drew Cerza. But the story of Buffalo's ascension to the top of the bar food chain starts long before Drew anointed himself Wing King for Life. But not as far back as you might think.

It's surprising to realize that the Official Appendage of Hooters is a very modern marvel, like Crocs or Bruce Jenner's new face. Before my visit to western New York, I never considered that wings had been "invented." I had assumed that, like death and tight pants on Thanksgiving, wings had been a delicious part of our national menu from the first chicken. But I was wrong.

In the beginning, the spicy delight we now know as "buffalo wings" were junk, no more than the uneaten chicken chum that got trashed. Until one day, during the turbulent '60s, a hungry kid and his clever mom forever changed the course of Western civilization. This is their story. . . .

Buffalo, New York, was founded in 1832 as the westernmost point on the Erie Canal. A stone's throw from Canada, the city has been America's frozen little toe ever since. If you've ever spent an overcast, winter day in Buffalo, you understand why bars are as important to the city as snow plows. When it's 30 below, the Bills have lost and the Sabres are on the West Coast, there's simply nothing else to do but drink.

To pass the hours, Dominic Bellissimo and his pals would hang out in his parents' bar, drinking beer and shooting pool—actual billiards, not Wii. Over many hours, and many pitchers, the physical act of shooting the balls around the table always led to hunger.

But one fateful night in 1964, Dominic and his buds didn't realize they were hungry until after the kitchen was closed. As panic set in, Dom did what any hungry Italian boy would do—he told his Ma to get into the kitchen and make somethin'.

Forty years later, the inspiration of that devoted matriarch has spawned a new cuisine, billions of pesky pants stains, and an annual pageant that provides much needed prize money to Hooters waitresses all over America—those nylons don't buy themselves.

> The inspiration of that devoted matriarch has spawned a new cuisine, billions of pesky pants stains, and an annual pageant that provides much-needed prize money to Hooters waitresses all over America—those nylons don't buy themselves.

But that night, Theresa Bellissimo, co-owner of Buffalo's world-famous Anchor Bar (the "Buffalo" part), walked into her kitchen, only to find her cupboards empty!

In her maternal panic, she realized all she had was leftover scraps from the chicken breasts she'd been preparing earlier (the "wings" part.) Back in the day, nobody ate the gristly chicken meat from below the knee. But her boys had the late night munchies, so in a moment of inspiration Theresa became a Mother Theresa of Invention.

She gathered her gristly bones, dropped 'em in the fryer, then doused them in an improvised hot sauce—a sauce sold at the bar ever since. She grabbed a bowl of ranch dressing, the only vegetable in reach, celery (in case the wings were too hot), and threw them all together in a bowl. Moments later, Dominic made history as the first dude to ever scream in pain after getting wing sauce in his eye.

For a long time, Theresa's husband Frank refused to put this strange, new recipe on the menu, fearing that it would harm the Anchor Bar's reputation for fine Italian cuisine. But Dom couldn't stop telling anyone who'd listen how great his mom's "wings" were. People came from all over the city to try these tasty oddities.

Over time, butchers realized their garbage cans were over-flowing with cash, and stopped throwing away their chicken junk, selling them as "wings" to bars and restaurants around the country. Kids like Dom would never go hungry again.

These wings from Buffalo were a bar owner's delight—cheap meat designed to be cooked in the very same fryers already churning out fries and fried cheese. It didn't take long for the mom and pop joints to be joined by national food chains in their love affair with the tasty wing.

Soon, like the Carolina barbecue wars of the early 50s, and the Supreme Court battle over whether the eleventh ingredient in the Colonel's secret recipe was an "herb" or a "spice," regional sauce conflicts ignited around the country. It was bar against saloon, chili against habañero in the quest for the best buffalo wing sauce. In her unknowing haste, Momma Bellissimo had created an industry. Sadly, precious few know her story. I'm doing my part by including her story in this bestseller. But more must be done to commemorate her contribution to America. But what . . . ?

Nothing short of a national holiday can properly recognize how wings have changed our lives. We've already got "Shark Week" every fall and "International Internal Audit Awareness Month" every May, why not honor buffalo wings? Screw Arizona if they refuse to celebrate it, the rest of us would welcome the day off, not to mention the funny Hallmark cards and office pools.

Tired of waiting for the other forty-nine states to get hip, in 2002 Buffalo chose Labor Day as THE day, and crowned wholesale wing salesman Drew Cerza as their king. Back on the infield, it's 96 degrees at 2:50 p.m., and Drew "Wing King"

My Favorite . . . BREAKFAST
The Loveless Café, Outside of Nashville, Tennessee

The Loveless Café is a converted Bates Motel–style roadside

motel that has become one of the busiest diners in America. Miss Carol Fay made biscuits and gravy at the Loveless longer than the new owners have known about its existence.

Made fresh every day, the Loveless still conjures up the best breakfasts in the country with two seemingly simple sides: biscuits and gravy.

COURTESY OF PAMELA SCHNEIDER

Miss Carol Fay passed away in April of 2010, only months after her retirement. Thankfully, a chosen one was trained by the Maestro herself so that the Loveless would continue her legacy. As it has been since the beginning, the biscuits come

COURTESY OF DANNY BATES/LOVELESS CAFÉ

first. Early every day the neophyte arrives before dawn to mix the dough, roll it out, and bake it up fresh in giant bread ovens. While the delicious scent of baking biscuits fills the air, the kitchen starts on the gravy—yet another closely guarded secret, though it seems to feature whole milk, bacon, bacon fat, and other delicious seasonings. They work the gravy to a simmer just in time to remove the biscuits hot from the oven.

If you time your arrival just right, you'll get the biscuits right out of the oven, covered with a fresh dollop of gravy from the eternally simmering pot.

If you doubt that something as simple as milky grease and bread can be the best breakfast in America, you obviously haven't been to the Loveless.

You haven't stood on the wooden porch, rubbing your belly as the morning dew burned off the tall grass, already wishing you were headed TO the Loveless, not away from it.

COURTESY OF MICHAEL STERN/LOVELESS CAFÉ

Only time will tell if the current biscuit-baker will admirably fill Miss Carol Fay's apron. If you find yourself anywhere close to Nashville, get off the big road and find out for yourself.

Cerza—the guy who filled the pool at dawn with every last bottle of blue cheese dressing in western New York—is now worried that today's intense heat might turn the goo "funky." Which is important because in ten minutes, eight shirtless, goggled frat boys will "bob" for wings, open-mouthed and of their own free will, through the fifty gallons of blue cheese dressing sloshing in the kiddie pool at second base.

The king stares blankly across his crowded kingdom. He's thinking back to that pivotal meeting when he convinced elected officials that the best way to promote their beloved Buffalo, and its profitable meat, would be mixing frat boys and cheese. Tough sell. But I watched Drew work his magic kingdom of one hundred thousand loyal subjects, preside over the National Chicken Wing Eating Championship, and convince eight buzzed mooks that their goo bobbing would be totally safe. "Trust me . . . I'm the Wing King."

God save the King! If it wasn't for Drew's impassioned cajoling, I would have never witnessed the grandest, grossest live spectacle ever conceived . . . and that includes the AARP production of *Oh, Calcutta.*

The 1st Annual Buffalo Wing Bob was Drew's crowning achievement. It was like your first prom kiss—something to be experienced in person, and on an empty stomach.

Which is why I didn't participate. I had spent most of my day roaming from booth to booth, chomping on buffalo wings from restaurants from all around the country. Wings are like Oreos and pistachios—you CAN'T eat just one.

For two days, every Buffalonian I met felt compelled to breathlessly tell me that the Anchor Bar Wings were GREAT. AWESOME! The BEST! UNREAL! I walked around that ball field all day, making sure I'd tried every other wing . . . before Anchor time. I assumed they'd be good, but good enough to taste a difference? Doubtful.

I got my Anchor basket and dug in . . . DAMN! Not greasy, succulent chicken, the blue cheese wasn't too mayonnaise-y, and the sauce blossomed on my tongue, front to back, just like it's supposed to! I love spicy food, and this sauce had the perfect blend of burn-your-hair HOT and subtle spicing. When the back of my neck sweats, I'm in heaven, and the Anchor Bar Wings had me banging on the pearly gates.

Drew's PA announcement woke me from my moist reverie and sent me sprinting toward the kiddie pool—it was BOB time. And because I was rollin' with Brian the cameraman, I'd be watching from the front row, with a hundred thousand of my newest friends cheering behind us.

It was twenty minutes I'll never forget.

The Bob began with eight shirtless dudes . . . who may have been drinking prior to competition. Though performance-enhancing chemicals are frowned upon during Olympiads and the Tour de France, they're pretty much essential for The Bob. The rules of The Bob require finalists to keep their hands behind their backs, their mouths open, and their noses plugged while bobbing through the Wishbone. The winner is the warrior who fishes the most wings out of the communal goo during their twenty-minute troll.

Damaged, semi-eaten, or perforated wings do not count. Each hidden wing must be scooped up with a "soft mouth," not unlike a Labrador, and deposited into a metal tray at the contestant's hip. A judge, licensed and bonded by the state, counts the intact wings and declares the winner.

> Each hidden wing must be scooped up with a "soft mouth," not unlike a Labrador, and deposited into a metal tray at the contestant's hip.

Such brave warriors! To battle so hard, for so long, they must be vying for a trophy like no other. Not an Oscar, or a Nobel, but a proper prize that proclaims to all the world . . . THE Wing Bob Champion! That prize could only be the ultimate modern totem of complete domination: a free t-shirt.

Listen to me now. I've seen more of America than the members (new and classic) of Molly Hatchet, REO Speedwagon, and Lynyrd Skynyrd combined. And I see a problem. Forget booze, pot, and meth. Our war on drugs will take care of those tiny problems in a jiffy.

COURTESY OF BRIAN MILLER

The REAL danger with these kids today is free, promotional t-shirts. They're everywhere, even within the Wing King's greasy kingdom.

No one understands t-power better than Cerza, who uses the dangle of a Wing King t-shirt to entice his bobbers to swap spit, sweat, and chicken bones. It's the Ultimate Fighting Championship in a wading pool of salad dressing, but at least Cerza makes sure it's a fair fight.

To begin the Bob, all eight shirtless mooks are stationed around the perimeter of the pool. They are told that beneath the opaque surface of the blue cheese dressing—which is completely safe, by the way—hundreds of buffalo wings (the King never refers to them as just "wings") have been hidden. The mook who can find and retrieve the most in the allotted time will be crowned champion.

The King blows his whistle and the Bob begins! The guys thrust their heads below the surface like pelicans diving for fish. Because their hands are tied behind their backs, they topple easily . . . which means within seconds, they are all waist-deep in goo. The technique that most seem to follow is an open-mouthed bottom crawl. Then, when their mouth encounters something they think might be a wing, they bite and rise back to the surface. With dressing dripping from their eyes, they turn to their tray and drop the wings in like well-trained bird dogs.

Despite the monarch's best efforts, the frenzied glory of sport quickly devolves into roller derby. One of the guys can't seem to come up with any wings on his own, so he resorts to biting them out of other guy's mouths as they surface. The King quickly whistles this uncomfortable spectacle to a stop, and the fair fight continues.

And what a fight! After twenty minutes of gargling communal goo and head-butting adversaries off a bone, one chicken hawk stood taller than the rest. With eighteen wings nestled safely in his tray, the King crowned his new champion . . . with a t-shirt.

Perhaps years from now, when all these gooey mooks are grown and are watching kids of their own slosh through some kind of futuristic nano-gunk, they'll feel the pride and sense of accomplishment they themselves were lacking. That's real change and, ultimately, what buffalo wings are all about.

> **After twenty minutes of gargling communal goo and head-butting adversaries off a bone, one chicken hawk stood taller than the rest.**

Twelve hours in the hot sun, consuming nothing but hot buffalo wings and cold beer, helped me realize that like Theresa Bellissimo, we can change the world.

Maybe one day soon, those drunken frat boys will be bobbing for the love of sport . . . and chicken meat, not the empty thrill of clever cotton.

That will be a Labor Day to remember.

BUFFALO-STYLE CHICKEN WINGS RECIPE

The Anchor Bar DOES NOT provide their buffalo chicken wing recipe. However, the following version is a good starting point for novices eager to bring a little bit of Buffalo home.

Makes 4 to 6 servings.

Blue cheese dressing (choose your favorite chunky bottled
  dressing)
24 (about 4 pounds) chicken wings
Salt and freshly ground black pepper
4 cups vegetable oil
4 teaspoons butter
2 to 5 tablespoons hot pepper sauce or to taste
1 tablespoon white vinegar
Celery sticks

1. Refrigerate blue cheese dressing first for 1 hour before using.
2. Cut off the tip of each chicken wing and discard it. Cut the
   wing in half (cutting at the joint) to make two pieces. Wash
   and dry the chicken wings. Sprinkle with salt and pepper.
3. In a deep fryer, add vegetable oil and heat to 400°F or until
   the oil starts to pop. If using an electric fryer, set the temperature to 425°F.
4. Add half of the chicken wings and cook 10 to 15 minutes
   or until golden and crisp, stirring occasionally. When done,
   remove from the hot oil and drain on paper towels. Repeat
   with second half of chicken wings.
5. In a large saucepan over medium heat, melt butter. Add
   hot sauce and vinegar; stir well and remove from heat immediately. Add drained and cooled chicken wings and mix
   together.
6. Using tongs, take chicken wings out of sauce and drain off
   excess sauce. Place the wings on a hot grill or in a 350°F
   oven for 2 to 3 minutes to bake in the sauce. Serve with
   blue cheese dressing and celery sticks.

Chapter 6
It's a Man's World

When I was a kid I couldn't wait for the summer vacation so I could stay up late and go out to the ballpark on Wednesday nights to watch my heroes. While my friends gawked over Ron Santo, Dick Butkus, or Phil Esposito, I reserved my reverence for Pete, Don, and Chris, my uncles. They were all-stars on various city championship teams from 1951 to 1985, Chicago's golden age of softball.

They weren't TV famous, just famous enough to sneak me into their local taverns for a sip of victory beer while they collected their winnings. Taverns are where I learned that it does matter whether you win or lose, especially if you go double or nothing. What's the difference between a "tavern" and a "bar"? About $2 a draft.

My uncles were the kings of the West Side. Uncle Christy, a pack-a-game powerhouse, could drill DeBeers softballs up, over, or through any fence in Chicagoland. A mobster played on Uncle Donny's team until he got cut—beyond recognition—by temperamental associates. But Uncle Pete was the shit. During the week he wouldn't talk if his hair was on fire and moved like he was dragging a piano behind him. But once he put on his shiny Wednesday night pants, he transformed like a superhero. He ran like a gazelle, pounced on balls like a cat, and hit the ball so hard the sound alone made fans flinch. He played in four decades and was inducted into the Chicago 16" Softball Hall of Fame in 2009.

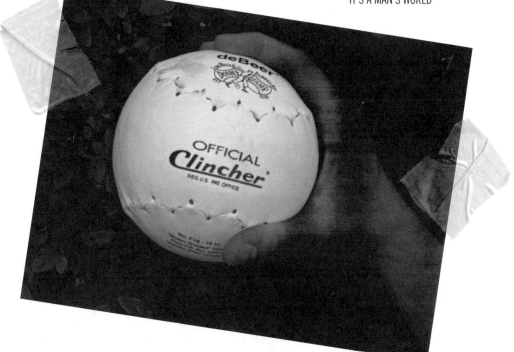

Sixteen-inch softball is a sports muta-
tion developed in Chicago before World War II as a
game played without expensive equipment, and on smaller fields
than twelve-inch softball. The bigger, heavier ball restricted the
distance a dinger would fly, so the games could be played on
vacant lots and inside gyms. If indoor softball sounds crazy,
you've never been to Chicago in January.

For some reason, The Game, as it's called in local taverns,
never spread out beyond Chicago. Maybe because, unlike the
twelve-inch game playable by guys named "Chad," "Jarrod," and
"Travis," the kind of guys who played sixteen-inch never used
gloves and always played for cash. "Chads" don't even play golf
without a glove.

Teams came out of ethnic neighborhoods and were named
for the factories the guys sweated in during the day or the taverns
in which they bullshat at night. Sixteen-inch can only be played

right by the kind of jags who work in factories and keep coolers stocked with Miller High Life in their trunks—just in case: the kind of mooks called "Stoogie," "Sweetwater," and "Eggs," because even after twenty years on the same team, nobody knows their real names. Drinking was mandatory, but restricted to the tavern, at least during playoffs. The only valid excuse for skipping postgame beers was if you or a blood relative ended up on the *Trib*'s obituary page the following morning.

All across the city, nobody played harder, or louder, than the Italians. At least that's how those summers seemed to me. We'd drive out to Melrose Park to watch my uncles pound the Polish, Irish, and German teams into the dirt. Hundreds of fans would cheer their fleshy faces and gnarled fingers as they whipped a pumpkin-sized rock around the infield faster than my eyes could follow. Playoff games in stadiums drew ten thousand paid, often dwarfing the attendance of the then dreadful Cubs and Sox. Sixteen-inch softball was Chicago's version of ethnic cleansing—and when you played the Italians, they'd clean you out.

You'd think that because the sixteen-inch ball is more massive than its effete twelve-inch cousin, playing with bare hands would be moronic. And you'd be right. Yet every night of the week at parks and stadiums around the city, blue-collar bombers braved screaming line drives and rocket-relay throws just to get the "W" . . . and the beer and cash attached to it. Sixteen-inch is fun when you win. When you don't, it just hurts. You can always tell a player by his fingers—if they look like they've been slammed in the trunk of an Eldorado, he's authentic. Another good tip-off is white socks and brown shoes at a wedding.

Sixteen-inch is group therapy for guys who would never, ever attend group therapy: a loud, boisterous activity, soaked

in beer and self-aggrandizement, and clothed in threads that chicks dig. In short, it's perfect.

But transcendent as sixteen-inch is, it only ranks second in the all-time pantheon of Man. First place is, and will always be, barbecue.

Barbecue

bar–b-cue. n. 1. Animal meat, chased and charred, prior to ingestion. 2. How Barbie shoots 9 Ball. v. 1. Relentless searing of weekend victuals, usually while drinking and complaining about bullshit.

Softball and barbecue are Two Horsemen of the Guypocalypse. Both require beer, synchronized movement, and cool uniforms/bibs. Both confer trophies, bragging rights, and hard to remove stains. And both restrict women to the sidelines . . . until it's time to drive us home.

Men have always been transfixed by the sounds and smells of sizzling meat. Perhaps barbecue is seared into the Y chromosome. I can't prove it, but twenty minutes after Man domesticated fire, I bet the guy from the cave next door barged in to complain "Mammoth being cooked all wrong."

Over time, this annoying syndrome spread from backyard cookouts to organized events, where hopeful men braved blazing coals all day to be vindicated or vilified by their neighbor's supposedly refined palate. Sure, eating charred flesh is exhilarating, but it wasn't enough. We needed a winner to celebrate, and losers to pity. Because it's a man's world, everything, even eating, needs a scoreboard.

For the record, I think the concept of "judging" food is ridiculous. Of all human sensations, flavor is the most subjective. Food is either bad—kills you, or good—you live. Everything in between is individual preference. "Taste" happens inside your mouth—can't get more individual than that.

The ultimate judgment in the barbecue world happens every fall in Kansas City as seventy thousand barbecue beasts from around the globe gather for the World Series of Meat: The American Royal Barbecue Invitational. It's America's premier sausage fest . . . in more ways than one.

The Royal has been a Kansas City tradition since 1899, hosting yearly livestock and horse shows, as well as bull riding and rodeo competitions. The Invitational takes over the entire fourteen acres of the Royal fairgrounds, and for three days is the world's largest barbecue event.

Royal organizers told us contestants usually begin gathering in the parking lot Friday afternoon to be ready for the competition Saturday morning. Friday nights evolve into a huge tailgate featuring cook-off winners from all over the world re-creating their award-winning chicken, brisket, pork, and sparerib recipes, all for the chance to be hailed as an Imperial Booftar of Carnivoria.

We arrived early and hungry (do NOT eat for a week before attending the Royal) expecting to find a smattering of tailgaters setting up Weber kettles and rubbing their meat. What we found was a temporary charcoal village filled with smoking trailers, portable cabanas, and its own system of government.

The sprawling Royal complex is located on the site of the original Kansas City Stockyard, down in a valley. Fully half the area is parking lot, and by 2:00 p.m. Friday, there were already hundreds of barbecue rigs up and smoking.

I've been a carnivore all my life, but the aroma that enveloped our car, clothes, and lenses was the most savory scent I'd ever snorted. Because the chefs invited to the Royal have all won regional or state competitions, by any empirical definition, we

COURTESY OF CHRIS MARKS

were huffing the best smoke in North America, except for the chronic Snoop Dog gets.

The immense parking lot is partitioned into twenty-by-twenty areas that all feature some kind of grill, camping chairs, tent, and the all-important bar. They are staffed with groups of friends who start cooking/drinking at dawn. Everyone wears matching t-shirts, and once their meat is placed on automatically rotating grills, they all have plenty of spare time.

Per Man's World rules, the key to championship barbecue is cooking "low and slow." By nightfall, teams were already six hours into cooking entries that weren't due until noon on Saturday. In most of the stalls, guys just stood around their grills, talking trash and watching the automatic rotisseries rotiss.

Because no man is an island, or can cook on top of one without help, chefs surround themselves with a handpicked team of uniformed meat-eaters, guys that can be trusted to slice, dice, protect, and deliver their thirty hours of work across the parking lot into the judges' tent without tripping or tasting along the way. With thousands of contestants crammed into the booths, t-shirts have evolved into the best way to keep the players straight.

At first, the prospect of covering a three-day cook-off did not fill me with glee. Really, how many times can you ask a guy about charcoal? But after less than an hour, I realized why the Royal is so beloved by its patrons. And why I will return as often as possible. It's not the steak, it's the sizzle.

> At first, the prospect of covering a three-day cook-off did not fill me with glee. Really, how many times can you ask a guy about charcoal?

Sure, the cook-off is important, but it only really matters to three guys out of thousands. The rest return each year because of the Royal's dirty little secret: the party. Unless you're a vegan, the Parking Lot Party is the most fun you'll ever have on a Friday.

We started walking the aisles at dusk, shaking hands and sampling entries, and were immediately accosted by Nuclear Dawg Balls (jalapeños stuffed with cheese and wrapped in bacon). Chefs The Big Dawgs insist you eat them GTM, grill to mouth, hot and whole, because they're evil, evil men.

The Dawgs worked the party in much the same way I'd tortured fourth grade classmates, with punchlines timed to send lunch through their noses. The Dawgs seemed quiet and harmless . . . until I popped one of their Balls into my mouth. But the moment my lips closed around their sizzling, cheesy, crunchy treat, The Dawgs gleefully erupted with some of the funniest, filthiest jokes I'd ever heard. But The Dawgs weren't after laughs;

My Favorite....STEAK HOUSE
Morton's Steak House, Chicago, Illinois

Save me your screams of horror, Vegans, but sometimes the only thing that satisfies is a good steak.

Local steakhouses around the country are always good for a whirl, but unlike other types of food, the dice you roll for those dinners can get quite large. When a meal for four tops out near $500, it's a little more difficult to take a chance on the savory for the sake of the authentic.

So, when you absolutely, positively have to have a great steak that very night, Morton's is the place.

True, as a Chicagoan, I am biased because Morton's was born in the Windy City. But compared to the other national chain steakhouses, there is no comparison.

Ruth's Chris Steak House has its possessives confused, and coats their meat in butter—pushing a rich meal over the top. Especially if you don't indulge in giant slabs of beef often, dipping it in butter when you do is a sure way to spend the rest of the night gurgling and miserable.

Benihana is more flash than flesh, and an iffy call if you are really starving.

The steak places that occupy the next tier down lose on ambience, wine lists, and style.

No, if you want a guaranteed fine night of dining, with a great bottle of wine and a delicious, perfectly prepared steak, it's Morton's or my house.

For starters, they feature USDA prime-aged beef. If you don't know the difference, you'll taste it. For some reason, which has something to do with the actual strands of the meat itself, older beef is better than newer beef—providing that it's stored correctly. Finding a raw piece of flank on the sidewalk is not the same as claiming one from a Morton's cooler.

Next, they cook the beef to order and medium means medium. What you taste is the meat, not a salty slurry of spices used to obscure a less-than-stellar slab.

But it's the hospitality, the ambience, and the feel of Morton's that puts it a cut above. It is both classic and comfortable, elegant and populist. You can order off their fantastic wine list, or bring your own special bottle—because they don't make you feel like an urchin if you'd rather pay a corkage fee. And even though Morton's has locations all over the country, each restaurant somehow captures the homey feel of their flagship Chicago location.

You walk through those doors, and you feel that they're really glad to see you—not just because they know you're gonna be dropping several bills for dinner, but because they know you'll enjoy every bite.

So, because every rule has its exception, the carnivore caveat to my "no-chain-restaurant rule" is Morton's.

they wanted tears of pain, which they got . . . along with hilarious visuals, with every punchline.

Every choked laugh squirted melted jalapeño cheese through my nose and down my chin, while lodging chunks of Dawg Balls in my nasal cavity. Each breath burned like the fire of a thousand suns. I screamed in pain as I frantically used the tinsely end of a discarded toothpick to pry spicy chunks of chili out of my nose, all while The Dawgs literally rolled on the asphalt, laughing like hyenas.

When several gulps of Corona had returned me to consciousness, I wasn't angry. I was awestruck. Realizing I was in the presence of greatness, we shook hands . . . and waited for the next rube to stumble into their trap. Not surprisingly, it's much funnier when a stranger is gasping for air and cursing the baby Jesus. And funnier still when it's your ninety-pound sound woman.

After drying our eyes and draining more beer, I continued across the parking lot to pull practice pork. Pulled pork is a southern dish rendered by cooking a whole pig, skin and all, low and slow, until the meat is so juicy and tender that it can be literally pulled by hand off the bone.

The danger in cooking pulled pork is that by the time you figure out you're doing it wrong, it's way too late to do anything about it. In an effort to avoid that kind of culinary catastrophe, many chefs get their rigs going early Friday, resulting in practice pork, a test snack before the real submissions are prepared. We had lots of it, and if there's a difference between practice and game-day pork, I couldn't taste it.

The Royal has always been notorious for intense competition. Each year, 1,500 chefs cook for long tables of judges, each rendering a number score for each recipe. Astoundingly, most years, the difference between medaling or not has been less than 1 percent. Which is exactly why the party is so important.

Even though all Invitational chefs have won a local cook-off just to get their bid, most Royal invitees don't stand a chance to wave the Golden Tongs. But that doesn't stop them from showing up. Like those first few episodes of *American Idol* each year, every guy with a squirt can of lighter fluid and a box of Ohio Blue Tips truly believes he can be The One . . . until he rolls into that parking lot crammed with 1,500 grills, most of which cost more than his house. That's when the smoky stench of reality smacks him in the face:

"Winning" an invite to the Royal: $50 judge's bribe.

Loading up on meat, beer, and a brand new "Because I'm the Cook, that's why!" apron: $300.

The expressions on these poor newbies as they drive onto the lot for this "casual" cook-off: Priceless.

Newbie teams reveal themselves before the first Kingsford briquette ashes over. Their booths have no style, no free samples, no open bar—just folding chairs, a grill, and a Coleman cooler filled with light beer. Yes, they're on the team, but their uniforms will never get dirty. All it takes is one lap around the lot for these neophytes to realize they are in way too deep.

The bulk of the revelers are the Pikers, returning guys who know exactly what kind of behemoth the Royal has become, but are cocky enough to believe they have a shot anyway. Pikers usually have a "special, secret" recipe, believe their local victory wasn't a fluke, and—like the four losers in every Oscar category—always murmur they're happy just to be nominated while secretly expecting to win.

Then there are the Chosen Ones, the small circle of Royal recidivists with enough plaques, hardware, and ribbons to open their own gift shop. These are the teams with nothing left to prove, who nonetheless return every year to go fork to fork with anyone naive enough to think otherwise. These are The Contenders.

Anyone with a custom grill is a Contender.

Anyone whose rig is bigger than a Prius is a Contender.

Anyone who needs more than a nightstand to display their trophies and is still sober after 6:00 p.m. is a Contender.

PHOTOS COURTESY OF LIBBY KLEBECK

I spotted Chris Marks from fifty yards away . . . the bright red of his crown was like a homing beacon. That, and his twelve-foot-long table crammed with glittering trophies, made him easy to find.

When Chris saw our camera, he immediately donned his cape and crown for a photo op, looking like the bastard son of Dracula and King Friday.

Chris is a Kansas City native who teaches barbecue for a living. He's been using his dad's recipe for over twenty years and has amassed enough hardware to quell any question as to his skills.

After an unprecedented eight championships, the Royal is his house. Chris showed me around his kingdom of trophies, charcoals, and ice-cold beer with the same comedic swagger my uncles had after a grand slam on the softball field. Or a really good finger-pull.

Chris wisecracked about the cool-under-pressure calm essential to winning barbecue events, and the versatility. To be crowned Grand Champion of the Invitational, a team had

COURTESY OF LIBBY KLEBECK

to beat over one hundred teams in all FOUR categories: Chicken, Ribs, Pork, and Brisket, and get the highest combined score from the judges. All of the Contenders have won at least one championship, and many have won more than five. He explained that Saturday is the Invitational and Sunday is the Open, which is why the party is Friday.

Contenders learn to balance the pageantry and the pork over the long weekend. His Highness knows that cooking low and slow means one fleeting moment of distraction can ruin an entire weekend of toil. And because they've all tasted champagne, Contenders also know that the drive home is a lot longer without a new trophy strapped in the passenger seat.

After watching him work for a while, I asked Chris to take us around and introduce me to all the wild characters he's met during his reign at the Royal. He loved the idea, but sent me solo. A few minutes of joking and spritzing was fine, but this wasn't a party, it was playoffs, and at 6:00 p.m., he was already running behind. As last year's reigning champ, he knew every sweaty, greasy grillmaster in this lot was gunning for him. And he wasn't about to give them a chance. After promising to spend more time tomorrow, he cocked his crown and turned back to his ribs. Heavy is the head upon which hangs the meat.

If NASCAR and the Pillsbury Bake-Off had a gigantic, greasy baby, it would be the Royal. It has no equal in size or scope, and the vibe is certainly more Midas than Martha Stewart. Obviously, we couldn't meet seventy thousand people, so I had to come up with a plan to quickly locate only the best of the best. This was a job for my Dining Divining Schnoz (DDS).

I happen to have a very good sense of smell. I can walk up and down the street, pausing just long enough for me to stick my nose inside the doorway of every restaurant. I get

> **If NASCAR and the Pillsbury Bake-Off had a gigantic, greasy baby, it would be the Royal.**

a lot of strange looks, but eventually, one place wins my nasal jackpot. When a place has a "loud" smell, it means the food is excellent. If it didn't smell enough, the food was tasteless and not worth our time. In four hundred cities, I don't think I picked more than five clinkers.

To save time, I adapted my DDS for the wide-open Royal by walking around with my eyes to the ground. I shuffled along without really looking, sniffing for a savory smell to lift my head. After a long time, my feet stopped at the base of a big, black hot rod, complete with painted flames and racing wheels. One whiff told me I had arrived.

This wasn't "Texas Johnny" Trigg's first barbecue. Johnny was already a celebrity back home in Alvarado, a barrel-chested, cartoonishly-Texas Texan, with a voice Foghorn Leghorn himself would covet. Like they do every year, Johnny and his wife "Mother" drove their Smokin' Triggers RV up from their Dallas suburb, dragging their flame-covered money-maker behind them.

You've gotta have a big pair of tongs to roll into The Royal with a tugboat like Trigg's. Luckily, Johnny does. And they're safely tucked away in Mother's purse. The Triggs have an ideal retirement, travelling the country competing in barbecue events, supplementing their small retirement checks with giant ceremonial checks on a regular basis. Smokin' Triggers have won over forty Grand Championships nationwide and are the only team that's ever won the prestigious Jack Daniel's Championship twice . . . so far.

Johnny is a Contender. Just ask him. While the Royal was ramping up to party-gear, Johnny and Mother just sat by their hot rod grill and smiled as the Pikers and Newbies gawked at their rig and whispered in reverence. They'd been down this asphalt before and knew nighttime at the Royal wasn't for boozing and cruisin'; it was all about the brisket.

Johnny graciously took the time to explain that brisket is cow shoulder and notoriously difficult to barbecue. It's the grand piano of beef: In the hands of an artist, it can delight like a Marcia Ball boogie-woogie. But in the hands of a pretender, brisket is atonal Chopsticks. The uninitiated typically falter by over-smoking the slab, thereby failing to retain the moisture that tenderizes the meat and amplifies its flavor. But those are my words. Johnny's actual response was more succinct.

"Too much is more'n it can handle."

During my long journey into this smoky night, Johnny also schooled me in barbecue's eternal conflict: Man vs. Meat. Some Contenders insist success is all about smoking and charring technique, while others explain that all that matters is the choice of cut. "When I'm competing," he told me with a straight face, "my trick is—I always make sure to buy the left brisket." Long pause.

Johnny was tweaking me. It's a Texas thing—they see how gullible you are, then mock you until you cry. The only way to gain a Texan's respect is to call their bluff—Texas Hold'em style. So I asked again, this time, mano a mano a meat.

Johnny leaned across the custom maple table that decorated the luxury RV that ran on the premium gas that Johnny bought with his barbecue winnings, and whispered his secret.

"You look at any cow lying in a field. Every time they get up, they do like this . . . " Johnny proceeded to mime a resting cow pushing its right leg forward and using it as a fulcrum to lurch up onto all fours. "Left side don't have to shoulder that load every day. 'Cause of that, the left side is always more tender, and better tasting."

Johnny looked me dead in the eye, without a hint of a smile. If he was serious, it was the dumbest thing I'd heard all day—including a mom telling her kid it was "okay" he struck out in softball. I laughed in Johnny's face.

Johnny didn't think that was too funny . . . which of course, made me laugh more. When I finally caught my breath, I hit Johnny with a withering series of professional host questions, sure to reveal whether he was full of bull.

How did he know all cows do that all the time? What if they all sit down with their left legs first? If the right muscle is always bigger, why aren't America's pastures filled with crooked cows?

He just shrugged and pointed to a wall filled with trophies. In the end, I couldn't tell if Johnny was messing with me or not. And it was too late to strap him to a polygraph. Besides, the Triggers were clearly tired of having me in their kitchen, and we had an early call the next day. I bid the Texans good night and headed out.

We met hours more characters and enjoyed pounds more meat before the giant block party started to wind down. By 1:00 a.m. the bands went silent, leaving the Pikers with visions of spareribs and sloppy bibs dancing in their heads.

I headed off to my car, then noticed that there was one set of work lights still burning over at Big Bob Gibson's. I hadn't had a sample of meat in over twenty minutes, so I swung by to get a pocketful for the ride back to the hotel.

Google "Contender" and Chris Lilly's picture will pop up. Though the rest of his Decatur, Alabama, team was already passed out by the time I showed up, this winner of ten world barbecue championships, including six prestigious Memphis in May world titles, was still hard at work rubbing spices into his butt. His chicken and ribs would wait until morning, but Chris's brisket and pork butt would need some massaging through the night to get them ready for their date with the smoker.

Chris didn't come here to party. He didn't come here to drink. Not once during the preceding six hours of pagan revelry had he even left the grill for a bathroom break. I'm all for low and slow, but at some point you got to go.

We rolled up on Chris, camera rolling, and I tried to get him to have some fun with us before the night slipped away, but he was not to be tempted. Chris Lilly wasn't interested in fun; Chris Lilly was back at the Royal to win. His business depended on it.

Big Bob Gibson's is a family institution in Decatur, and Chris, as the great-grandson-in-law of Big Bob himself, was the patriarch, a job he did not take lightly. He had married into the Gibson family years ago, but rather than accept an instant offer to run the restaurant, Chris insisted he start at the bottom and work his way up. That meant showing up before dawn with the meat guys, to prepare the hundreds of slabs they'd cook up each day. Chris learned the art of barbecue from the old-timers who'd put Big Bob Gibson's on the map, and didn't take over until he knew what he was doing. That dedication to the physics and philosophy of "the rub" put Chris in a league of his own.

Chris's focus and articulate attention to detail were rare, but after twelve hours of revelry, I was well done. I had just enjoyed

My Favorite... FRIED CHICKEN

Gus's Fried Chicken, 310 S. Front Street, Memphis, Tennessee

They don't give kitchen tours at Gus's.

They don't share their recipe at Gus's.

Do NOT go to Gus's if you are in a hurry, or if you require waiters to fawn over your every desire. The Gussers and Gussettes don't give a crap. The service is pleasant, but slow, due in no small part to the crush of carnivores that descend on this cinder block shack every day at feeding times.

It ain't the ambience. It ain't the service. It ain't the communal seating. It's the Chicken. Throughout the fifty states, the District of Columbia, AND Puerto Rico, Gus's is my FAVORITE FRIED CHICKEN in America.

And not just me: every member of the crew agrees. It's so light, spicy, and crispy on the outside, and juuuuicy on the inside, we broke our "one-time" rule . . . we had Gus's chicken three days in a row. And stopped on our way out of town for more!

And not because they loved having the Travel Channel crowding into their forty-by-forty cell block. They didn't want us to shoot. They didn't want to be on our Web site. They wouldn't even let us into the kitchen to watch. They didn't offer me a free t-shirt—I had to pay for it! That's the showbiz equivalent to slapping me across the face with dueling gloves. They took us for granted, but we loved them anyway.

If you're in Memphis and had your fill of the dry rub ribs at Rendezvous, head down to the river, to the diner that turns chicken into moans of pleasure. Tell 'em Mark sent you . . . they'll ignore you.

one of the most hilarious, delicious, and raucous nights of my life. The Royal tailgate delivers the perfect slurry of food, music, and characters. On second thought, even vegans could have had some laughs. Who doesn't love deep fried corn on the cob . . . if it's fried in vegetable oil?

I returned Saturday morning to a different Royal. The jovial camaraderie was gone, and each stall was locked in a life or death struggle to cook, plate, and transport their four entries: chicken, ribs, brisket, and pork, across the complex to the judging building every half hour on an exact timetable. One minute late, and the entry would be turned away, dashing any hope of an overall victory.

Big Bob's tent was humming like a M*A*S*H unit. Chris finished the meats, arranged them in the Styrofoam to-go boxes on top of garnish, then handed them off to a uniformed runner who galloped across the lot to submit. There was no time for interviews; we just stood off to the side and watched the ballet.

Chris Marks was in full regalia as he emptied his grill amid the controlled chaos of his very hung over crew. A few pieces hit the asphalt instead of the garnish, but there was plenty more, no doubt a lesson learned the hard way. The extras were carefully arranged as Chris's wife waved her magic bell over the boxes and Chris sent his entries off to meet their eaters.

The Smokin' Triggers got up early, had their coffee, and were calmly assembling their entries as frenzy exploded around them. Johnny's secret weapon was neatly arranged in the box before they put some Texas mojo in it for luck. Unlike most of the teams, it was just the two of them on final approach, and they clearly had a system. Their final entry was due at high noon, and breezed onto the judge's table with thirty seconds to spare.

Then, like on the Seventh Day, at 12:01 p.m. the Royal rested. Until the awards were announced in the amphitheater at 3:00

p.m., thousands of more than interested bystanders could only wait. And eat the leftovers.

After thirty-six hours of nonstop booze, brews, and barbecues, there was nothing else to do. A nervous quiet draped over the valley like a body bag, as competitors shuffled from booth to booth, sampling scraps and mentally comparing them to their own entries. Music played soft and mellow, like a hospital waiting room, as a parking lot full of Contenders waited for The Announcement.

The stands of the amphitheater were packed long before the Royal announcer took the stage. After what must have seemed like an eternity of preamble and kudos, he got down to business. After a slew of lesser awards, it was finally time to learn who had accumulated the highest combined score for all four of their meats to be crowned Royal Overall Champion.

Third place . . . Smokin' Triggers from Alvarado, Texas. Johnny lurched up—on both legs—and lumbered down the bleachers to claim his trophy.

Second place . . . Head Country II from Oklahoma. My DDS failed me here, because we had no idea who these guys were. But if they still had leftovers, I'd change that in a hurry.

And first place overall . . . Chris Lilly at Big Bob Gibson's! Chris got his confetti shower, a slap on the back from a guy in a cow suit, then made a gracious acceptance speech. As the stands slowly emptied, Chris walked his trophy back to the stall to start packing up for the long ride home. His weekend of hard work had paid off.

"What are you gonna do now?" I asked him as he cleaned his grill rack with steel wool.

"Take some time off," he smiled. "Just relax, eat my wife's cookin', and have some fun."

I wonder what he means by fun? You think Big Bob's sponsors a softball team?

CHRIS MARKS'S THREE LITTLE PIGS CHAMPIONSHIP RIB RECIPE
Kansas City Sticky Ribs

4 (2-pound) slabs baby back pork ribs

1 cup regular yellow mustard

4 cups Three Little Pigs Sweet Rub

2 cups melted salted butter

4 cups honey

1 bottle Three Little Pigs Competition BBQ Sauce

1. Heat smoker to 250°F using natural lump charcoal, add 2 chunks of either apple- or cherry-flavor wood once the charcoal is ready to go.

2. Select 4 slabs of pork baby back ribs; strip membrane off back of each rib to guarantee tenderness. Liberally coat yellow mustard over both sides of the baby back rib; this will act as a tenderizer and a bonding agent for the rub.

3. Meanwhile, select your favorite barbecue rub and coat both sides of the ribs. I prefer Three Little Pigs Kansas City Sweet Rub for Ribs.

4. Place ribs in a vertical rib rack for 5–6 hours depending on your smoker. Halfway through the cooking time rotate the ribs 180 degrees in the rack. This will guarantee an even cook.

5. Once the meat has pulled back from the bones, use a toothpick to check tenderness.

6. Remove from rack and place flat on the smoker, and apply a glaze of butter, honey, and Three Little Pigs Competition BBQ Sauce to both sides of the rib.

7. Place the ribs back on the smoker flat, allow 15 minutes to heat the glaze and sauce, and then cut and serve hot.

Chapter 7
Awful Tasty

My mother's mother, aka my maternal grandmother, aka my Nani, was an Italian cook like ya read about. Della Serritella emigrated from Reggiano, Italy, through Ellis Island with her mother. They came over in steerage in 1912 with two suitcases, a favorite coat, and centuries of recipes stashed inside notoriously hard heads. They made their way to Chicago and settled on Monitor Avenue near some relatives: very near. There were three apartments in a row, and all nine floors housed relatives. There were over fifty cousins, aunts, uncles, and spouses crammed into those three adjacent buildings, all of them related but in ways too numerous and tenuous to explain here.

Italians, like most of the ethnic groups in that great pre-war influx, gathered in neighborhoods and brought their customs and lifestyles with them. They worked and played with the other immigrants, but returned to their own fiefdoms at night, neighborhoods known by the streets that housed their best bars and restaurants.

The Italians settled at Roosevelt Road and Halsted. The Germans dug in on Lincoln between North Avenue and Lawrence. The Irish, including the Daley family, settled on the South Side in and around Bridgeport. And the Jews settled Kedzie, south of Roosevelt, and ran the bargain bazaars on Maxwell Street. My great grandmother, a stereotypical little, old Italian lady, learned to speak fluent Yiddish buying her produce off the horse-drawn carts that circled the neighborhoods. Before every school year, she'd take my Uncle Don and my dad shopping for clothes.

"Keep your mouths closed, and pick out what you like," she'd whisper to the boys as they approached the multitude of clothing racks that lined the sidewalks. The Jewish shopkeepers were so flattered she'd bothered to learn their language, they practically gave their suits away. Thanks to their grandmother, my dad and Uncle Donny were the only twelve-year-olds walking around in $150 silk suits. Bada Bing!

For the most part, the European tribes lived harmoniously in Chicagoland. The only rancor between Chicago neighborhoods sprang from their softball teams and their smell. According to Uncle Donny, the Italians had the best of both.

Monitor Avenue ("MON-itr AV-nyu") was good to the Italians and they multiplied, often eight to ten times. Della had eleven siblings, one of whom introduced her to one of Pete Rocco's twelve siblings, who then introduced her to Pete, an exotic foreigner . . . because he lived on the NORTH side of Roosevelt Road, the Italian equivalent of living on the far side of Saturn. They married, twice, once in City Hall, then again in church, and had five children; their youngest daughter, Angela, married Dan DeCarlo. Dan and Angela met in the alley the day the DeCarlos moved in behind the Rocco house.

Columbus crossed thousands of miles of rolling seas to discover the New World, but Chicago Italians refused to leave the block. By the time I arrived, Nani's sauce was famous for the 12 square blocks centered at Roosevelt Road and Austin Boulevard —our known Universe. Her homemade ravioli made old men weep and her pork neck-bones guaranteed perfect attendance at

Sunday dinners, where her Italian bread soaked up more sauce than an Irish wake.

As a kid, weekends at Nani and Papa's house were bookended by joyrides with Auntie Cookie and boredom from Lawrence Welk and *Mannix*. In between . . . we ate. Breakfast was eggs and sausage inside Italian bread. Lunch was homemade minestrone, pasta, sandwiches, and ginger ale from Silver Spring glass bottles. In between we had tomatoes and chunks of cheese the size of my head, but the nougat-center of my Nani-verse was a dented cookie tin on the middle shelf in the back pantry.

It didn't look special. Red with poinsettias, it was probably originally a Christmas gift, but over time became a touchstone of every holiday, event, and weekend spent in that house. It was always the first place I went when I walked through the door, and my last stop on the way out. There were two things seven-year-old me knew for sure: The sun would come up tomorrow over the statue of Mary, the Blessed Virgin Mother of God at the base of the backyard pear tree, and there would always be cookies in that tin.

Her homemade ravioli made old men weep and her pork neck-bones guaranteed perfect attendance at Sunday dinners, where her Italian bread soaked up more sauce than an Irish wake.

Sometimes I'd snatch a Chips Ahoy, other times a fistful of Oreos. For fun, I'd sometimes reach in without looking and pull out my prize—but whether it was a Tagalong jackpot or a Maurice Lanell virtually chipless chocolate chip, my fingers never touched bottom. In fact, I'm not really sure the tin had a bottom. It could have been a mystical portal, a black chocolate hole to another dimension where baked goods were as common as marginal Cub infielders. That, or she filled it up with cookies from the Jewel grocery when I wasn't around.

Regardless, Nani's attention to culinary detail and magic stove provided years of sanguine serenity I assumed every kid in America enjoyed. All grandmothers spent their weekend smooching cheeks and filling bellies with delicious food, right?

Wrong, especially when those grannies lived in Madison, Minnesota, the lutefisk capital of the USA. It was there, on a prairie that stays frozen longer than a beauty queen's smile, that I realized how lucky I'd been.

This eternal truth was revealed to me after our arduous trek to Madison, a charming town located just far enough into the two-lane hinterland to ensure ravenous hunger upon arrival, which would have been great had we been en route to Sausage and Peppers Fest. But we were headed to Norsefest, to watch Lutherans try to eat more lutefisk than other Lutherans, in front of a churchful of nauseous Lutherans.

Though fun to say with their accent, lutefisk is hard to swallow. Lutefisk is cod, soaked in cool water for six days, then soaked in caustic lye soda four more days. And not because, "Ooops, we dropped the fish in poison by mistake, but it's all the food we've got until the glacier thaws, so we better make the best of it, ya hey dere." Nope. The soaking is done on purpose to "lute" the fish, causing it to swell and bloat until you can poke your finger through it—as long as you're wearing welding gloves. The fish is then removed from its chemical bath and baked until done. A traditional lutefisk meal includes beer and aquavit . . . though not always permanently. Lutefisk has the highest chow down/ throw up ratio in the industrialized world.

Madison held its first Norsefest back in 1972, and crowned their first Lutefisk Queen in 1974. They have lutefisk cookouts every weekend. They erected Lou T. Fisk, a twenty-five-foot fiberglass cod in Jacobson Park. They sell t-shirts, buttons, and hats every November during Norsefest. They love their lutefisk . . . kinda.

The truth is, the "Lutefisk Capital of the USA" hates lute-fisk. Well, they don't hate it. But nobody seems to really like it. That's the dirty little secret I discovered from Ivey Vonderharr, the once and reigning Lutefisk Queen.

COURTESY OF IVEY VONDERHARR

I met Ivey at the giant fish in the park. She was dressed in Wagnerian regalia, complete with yellow pigtail wig and Elmer Fudd helmet. Ivey was crowned Ms. Lutefisk in 1974, but because festival organizers never got around to staging another contest, she was never forced to relinquish her crown, which is why she's been the only Lutefisk Queen Madison's ever known. And perhaps why they LOVE her.

In Madison, it was all about Ivey. It was like walking around Mayberry with Aunt Bee. Everyone just had to stop Ivey to thank her for something. She raised money for the schools, she helped the chamber of commerce, she raised money for the basketball team. With my own eyes I saw a crowd of well-wishers trample Mother Teresa just to get to Ivey.

There's lots of reasons to love this particular Viking. Her smile is radiant, her accent infectious, and her stories hilarious. I kept expecting her face to unzip so that Garrison Keillor could squeeze out. She has a robust laugh and used it plenty as she led me around, living her big life in that small town. We eventually fought past her groupies and made our way to the American Legion for the "Norsefest Lutefisk and Turkey Dinner" so I could finally experience real Norwegian-cooked fish.

But Ivey explained that nice German parishioners (not Norwegians) had worked since last Sunday to make enough lutefisk to feed the entire town. Before dinner, she took me back to the kitchen and introduced me to Mary Ann Moen, the head chef. Mary Ann was in charge because she was louder than her two boisterous friends. I asked her how they prepared the lutefisk, then sat down for the show.

"First, you soak the fish in lye for three days," she explained as she wrestled the slippery fish from pan to pan. "Then, soak it in water for another three days. Then, take an ovenproof dish and smear butter all over the inside. Then you take about three pound fish and lay the fish skin down in the dish and put salt all over it about one tablespoon. Then you cover the dish with foil and put in the oven set at 400 degrees for about thirty or forty minutes or until fish is flaky. Then you pour off the liquid and serve with boiled potatoes and lefse and melted smear. Is good."

Her kitchen was filled with cod pieces—for dinner, not dancers. The lutefisk was stuffed into pans on the table, in bowls on the counter, on plates in the fridge. The smell was deafening. Imagine if you can the stench of boiling batteries and butter. The noxious fumes filled the cramped kitchen and the Germans were getting a contact high. They told dirty jokes and laughed like sailors as they sloshed flaking chunks of fish out of the pans and into serving trays. When we'd all caught our breath after hearing the one about The Two Nuns that ends, "Twenty bucks, same as downtown!" I asked Mary Ann why she liked to eat lutefisk so much.

> Imagine if you can the stench of boiling batteries and butter. The noxious fumes filled the cramped kitchen, and the Germans were getting a contact high.

"I don't."

"If you don't like it, why do you eat it?"

"I don't."

"Ever?"

"We're German, not stupid." And so it began. "We cook it every year, dat way all of dem can get together and have dere party. But we don't eat it, no."

"Why?"

"Ya smell that? It don't taste no better."

"But the hall is full," I observed. "Why would this dinner sell out every year if people don't like the taste?"

"Go ask dem . . . and leave da door open, smells like a submarine toilet in here."

COURTESY OF MARY ANN MOEN

The dining room of the Legion was stuffed with Norwegian families having the time of their lives . . . I think. They're so taciturn, it's hard to tell if they've just won the lottery or lost a puppy. I talked to seniors, toddlers, and everyone in between. In a basement of three hundred Norwegians who'd each paid $15 to dine in jailhouse splendor, not one could look me in the eye and say they actually, really enjoyed the taste of lutefisk.

All around the room, plates were piled high with boiled potatoes, garlic toast, peas, and turkey. And exiled off to the

side, in a small, lonely yellow plastic bowl filled with melted butter, sat slivers of lutefisk. Everybody took a smidge, but nobody was eating.

When we arrived at fireman Tom's table, he twitched, like he'd been yanked out of his cell on death row. He dutifully forced a smile, then reached a trembling fork over to his lutefisk bowl. He speared a morsel . . . then snuck a look back to see if we were still there. We were. He tried to start up a conversation, the lute-fisked fork dangling between the bowl and his mouth. I demurred. Video first, then chit-chat. Tom gulped hard, then took

COURTESY OF MARY ANN MOEN

a microscopic bite. He made a yum-yum face and froze, but we wouldn't pan away until he swallowed. He finally did, then almost became a statistic. His stomach convulsed, his eyes bugged . . . then he took a deep breath and smiled—on-camera crisis averted. Then he held out a forkful to his kids, "Hey, you wanna be on TV?"

"No way!" they screamed and ran away.

And so it went. Two hours of "In the old country . . . " and "Our traditions . . . " but not one of them smiled with a mouthful of lye-soaked cod and credibly pretended they were lovin' it. Even Ivey couldn't motivate her masses, though she herself never stopped saying how much she loved the taste, the texture, and how she was sure I'd love it too. I promised her I'd eat as soon as we found someone without yarn-for-hair who'd back up her story.

Until then, the real story was that Madison was in denial. Sure, they sold the t-shirts and mugs and threw the parties, but nobody ate the fish. They got together every November to publicly pile the fish onto their plates . . . they just never bothered to eat it.

Why continue the charade? Anyone who'd be offended by the repudiation of this slimy delight was long dead. Maybe one hundred years ago Norwegian immigrants didn't know any better. But by the time the thirty-second annual Norsefest rolled around, even the worst convenience store burrito in town qualified as a better culinary mascot. Quaint was losing the war to edible. And Ivey knew it. She put on her brave face, but even the Queen couldn't prevent her subjects from eating . . . angel food cake. But she wouldn't give up. She promised to introduce me to at least one person who literally can't get enough lutefisk. He was over at the Prairie Arts Center preparing for the main event: the Lutefisk Eating Competition.

The bike rack outside the P.A.C., a converted church on a residential street, was choked with unlocked bikes as we made our way into the sold out show. We found the contest's reigning champion loitering nearby, intimidating, by his mere presence, the kids planning to challenge his crown. For over a decade, Jerry Ostermaas had outlasted everyone foolish enough to challenge him, and now he was making sure these ruffians knew all the gory details. Making sure everyone learned how he was the only contestant last year who didn't get sprayed with "vomitus." He also explained how his special

My Favorite . . . SOUP

Moose Head Soup, Anchorage, Alaska

Before snowmobiles and ski lifts, the hearty people of Alaska lived an even more isolated existence than they do today. It wasn't uncommon to live hours from the nearest store . . . and that was during the fifteen minutes of summer. In the long winter months, just finding food to put on the table was a full-time job.

So they hunted: deer, elk, and the belly-filling jackpot, moose. A single 1500-pound moose fed a family all winter long. But they were hard to hunt, and there was no guarantee that you'd ever bag another. That's why the locals use every part of the animal for sustenance. Moose tongue is a delicacy, but for the truly thorough hunter, nothing beats moose head soup.

Made from just the skull meat, moose head soup was the best way to utilize this particularly gamey, stringy meat to provide protein during the dark days of winter. Think minestrone, but instead of light chunks of USDA chicken, substitute moose face jerky. The soup has an oily, gamey taste, and is thick like a gumbo. It's not the most tasty soup I've ever had, and I'm not even sure I liked it the one time I had it. But there's just something about the idea of moose head soup that is triumphant and life-affirming.

Somewhere in the dark corridors of history, some Inuit—some hungry Inuit—decided to pull meat off the head of a dead moose and eat it, rather than starve to death.

And for THAT guy, that desperate, crazy dreamer, I salute the moose head soup makers and eaters of Alaska. Get yourself a bowl . . . if you're ever starving in Alaska. You Betcha!

eating outfit—they weren't lederhosen exactly—helped him maintain a steady eating pace until everyone else had stopped, dropped, and rolled.

Just an eating contest would be boring, so DJ and host Maynard Meyer combined his own mix of music, raffles, and talent show to keep things moving. The night started out with ten eaters on stage seated behind a long table filled with pans of lutefisk. The smart-aleck punks and seemingly lucid grownups shared one goal—the de-coronation of Jerry.

"The trays have been weighed. Each contestant will eat what they can," Maynard explained, "and when they're done, their pans will be weighed and the difference will become their official score. Eaters cannot leave the table, you can't stop eating. If you feel like you're gonna be sick, the bathrooms are just off stage. Because of what happened to Anders Olaff last year, we put some buckets under the table, but we don't have enough for everyone, so share if ya gotta. The contest will go until there's only one eater left. One, Two, Three—GO!"

The eaters tore into their lutefisk like it was actual food . . . and they did it on camera! Almost immediately, the frenzy of the competition gave way to a group-woozy, as everyone but Jerry took a communal breath to keep from making the front page of tomorrow's *Lake Region Times*. After a tense but successful pause, the carnage continued. When Maynard was sure there'd be no immediate casualties, he introduced the first talented act of singing sisters.

In the middle of the song, Maynard raced on stage to administer his first triage of the night. One of the smart-alecks at the end of the table was wobbling, and needed help exiting the stage. Sadly, the song was one verse too long. Here's a helpful hint for

parents dealing with rebel-lious teens: Nothing wipes off that smirk faster than little chunks of their own bile.

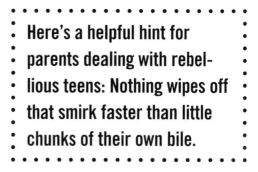

Here's a helpful hint for parents dealing with rebel-lious teens: Nothing wipes off that smirk faster than little chunks of their own bile.

For the next forty-five minutes, the "entertain-ment" alternated between the talents of charming kids and the grandeur of projectile fish barf. Far from shocked, the twinkle in Maynard's eye told me that this was exactly the show he planned: *Messy American Idol.* He's a showman, but no businessman. He let everyone in for free: big mistake. These same people just paid $15 for food they only pretended to eat. Imagine what they'd pay for a show they'd actually watch.

And they did watch. They whooped it up for every act until the last challenger dropped, leaving the still undefeated Jerry bloated and grinning at center stage. At no time during the com-petition did Jerry waver or gurgle. He took his time, enjoyed his record eight pounds of cod, and defended his title at a tortoise pace. Afterwards, I fought through a crush of lute-groupies to ask Jerry why he still pushed himself after all these years.

"I like the taste." Jerry's leathered face wrinkled into a wistful grin as he dabbed his shirt with a napkin. "Just like my grand-mother used to make it." His voice cracked a bit, then he used the napkin on his eyes.

Jerry's quote hit me like Thor's thunderbolt! These Nor-wegians weren't crazy. They weren't weird-talking, sleet-loving robots. They were human beings, and they loved their grand-mothers too.

Some of us are lucky enough to be born into Sunday dinners of sausage and peppers and ravioli, or picadillo, or brisket; others make do with boiled potatoes and soaked cod. And if that's all you know, you don't know enough to not like it, you know? But after you've seen the world, maybe even been to the Twin Cities, to continue eating lutefisk just because you've always done it is insane. Right?

But Jerry didn't look crazy to me. Nuts maybe, but not crazy. As I puzzled over why he was still breathing, Ivey walked up cradling a yellow bowl like it held the Secret to Life itself.

I'd avoided the goo at the Legion, at the Contest, at every opportunity all day long, but I'd finally run out of excuses. Ivey had spent eight hours squiring me around town, singing Viking songs, all without ever taking off her helmet or wig. Ten minutes after we met it felt like we'd known each other since Leif Ericson discovered the New World. Regardless of how nasty this stuff was— and it was—I just couldn't rebuff her advances any longer. It was lutefisk time.

> **Regardless of how nasty this stuff was—and it was—I just couldn't rebuff her advances any longer. It was lutefisk time.**

To ease my fears, Ivey took the first bite, leaving only a sliver of the slime resting on her fork for me to savor. Jerry and Ivey held their breath. I hoped to hold my lunch.

Slurp! I ate lutefisk. I swallowed lutefisk. But I didn't spew lutefisk.

At first, it burned my tongue. The flakey consistency of the fish dissolved on my tongue like the loogies of a thousand

hobos. The butter made it palatable, but didn't make it taste "just like lobster" as Ivey had promised. It tasted like something you'd force-feed a ten-year-old for screaming a few of George Carlin's "Seven Dirty Words" during quiet-time in church. I tried to chew it before it slid down my throat, but couldn't. The morsel dropped down my gullet like a dead parakeet into a toilet.

I opened my eyes to see Ivey's expectant face. Her hands were wringing her yarn pigtail, wondering, hoping that I'd enjoyed the Norsk Gold she'd just fed me. I looked at her across the bowl and tried to swallow away the greasy fish trail coating my tongue. Her eyes sparkled.

Then the strangest thing happened. My entire face smiled. Not on purpose or to make her feel good. Not because my hunger had been sated.

I smiled because in her beaming face, just for an instant, I saw my Nani's expectant look of pure pleasure smiling back at me over a steaming bowl of ravioli.

Lutefisk, Ya.

LUTEFISK FROM SCRATCH

Feeds: 10 people
Time: about 2 weeks
Reason: no good one

1 kilogram dried fish
30 liters of water, divided
100 grams caustic soda

To Prepare Lutefisk:

1. Saw the fish into pieces or leave it whole. Put the fish in water, and leave it in a cool place for 5 or 6 days if cut in pieces, 8 days if the fish is whole. Change the water every day.

2. For the luting use a stainless steel or enamel tub. Place the fish in the tub with the skin side up. Dissolve caustic soda in the water, yeah, caustic soda, pour it over the fish until covered completely by the lute water. Leave the fish in a cold place for 3–4 days.

3. When the fish is completely luted, it will be swollen and you can put a finger through it. Rinse the fish and leave in cold water 4–6 days. Change water every day.

4. If the fish stays in water for too long after the luting, it may be soft and difficult to boil. Test boil a piece, before company comes over. Do not make lutefisk in the warm season. 1 kilogram dry fish makes about 5 kilograms lutefisk.

To Cook Lutefisk:

1. Take an ovenproof dish and smear butter all over the inside.

2. Then take a fish weighing about three pounds and lay the fish skin down in the dish; put salt all over it, about one tablespoon.

3. Cover the dish with foil and put in the oven set at 400°F for about thirty or forty minutes or until fish is flaky.

4. Then pour off the liquid and serve with boiled potatoes and lefse and melted smear. Open windows and serve.

Chapter 8
The Idea of Pickles

The sweltering summer after high school graduation I worked as a glorified stock boy at the premier ladies' shoe store in suburban Chicago, Chernoff's Shoes. On the glamour scale, we were below Nordstrom's, but above Payless. On the bathroom scale, we catered to discerning ladies of all shapes and sizes, mostly plus, and we did it on commission.

There were usually four salesmen at a time, working in rotation. I stood at the front of the store, welcoming women and calling the next salesman over the microphone. Our salesmen were itinerant cutthroats too shady to sell used cars. Tom wore ill-fitting suits with black cowboy boots, Craig was a Miami Vice wannabe and wore tight fitting t-shirts with his shiny suits, and Roy was pasty thin and so jittery he could barely work the Brannock Device.

Charles Brannock invented the now ubiquitous metal measuring machine in 1927 as a way to help his dad's shoe store in Syracuse, New York, get a leg up on the competition. Prior to 1927, a clumsy wood device could approximate foot sizes, but was far from accurate when it came to determining widths from AAA to EEE. I know this because the owner of Chernoff's Shoes would quiz me on all things shoe-related whenever he saw me. And he saw me plenty.

Meyer Grumbakin was the ladies' shoe king of Chicago. Three hundred pounds but only 5'6", Meyer never appeared in public without a custom-tailored three-piece suit and his off-the-rack toupee. Meyer had the smooth of Barry White, the style of Baron Hilton, and the Hasidic charm of Zero Mostel, all neatly rolled into a snugly fitting Brooks Brothers casing. There were actually two shoe-selling machines at Chernoff's, the Brannock and the Grumbakin.

Meyer loved women, but not in a perverted, "stop staring at me" way. His secret was he enjoyed them. He always complimented clients—they were always "clients" with Meyer—on their scent, their apparel . . . and of course their feet. He was a master at faking sincerity, perhaps because he wasn't really faking. He had an innate understanding of the female psyche that he leveraged to finance his lavish lifestyle. His big white Cadillac had a Star of David air freshener hanging from the mirror; he wore three gold rings on his "measuring hand," and somehow found suits louder than his booming voice.

Unlike the rest of the guys who gambled in the back until I called them out for a client, Meyer would stand next to me and observe the store with grandfatherly contentment while he waited for his next ingénue. He'd quiz me about brands and types of shoes, famous Americans, and math. He took a keen interest in my college plans, and I enjoyed hearing his rambling, truly hilarious stories. On slow days, we'd stand up there for hours, just shooting the shit. It was like stealing money. But when things were jumping, it was all business. When he was having an especially productive day, he'd point out women around the store and predict their purchases, just to show off.

"Brown purse," he'd whisper as his lower lip curled down to his chin. "Cole-Haan slingback, 6½ B, brown, taupe, and black. Cankles, over in the corner, Nine West pump, the Palm Beach,

8 EE, in black and navy . . . " When one of the ladies noticed our attention, he'd smile and bellow across his store.

"May I help you, daaaaahling?"

"No thank you," they'd coo. "Just looking."

The lion would chortle, then saunter over to separate the gazelle from the herd. In no time, "Just Looking" would need help carrying boxes to her car. Meyer would give me the sign, and I'd whisk the stack out to her trunk and politely refuse a tip . . . because he'd always slip me two silver dollars when I came back. But even my tips were all business.

It started one day when I was back in the stacks, sorting shoes. Roy burst through the curtain and threw his stack of boxes against the wall.

"This fucking broad is driving me CRAZY!"

"What size?" Meyer said, without looking up from his lunch.

"10D. But every pair I put on her fat fucking feet, she says they make her look fat. YOU ARE FAT, LADY! What do you want me to do about it?"

"I'll handle it." Meyer picked up the shoeboxes and Roy dashed over to the vending machine for another Pepsi with a Lucky Strike chaser. From the corner, I watched Meyer pick up the 10D pump, wet his thumb, then rub off the size stamp from the inside back of the shoe. Then, very carefully, he took the black pen he always carried in his vest and wrote something in its place. I walked up behind him.

"What are you doing, Meyer?" He jumped, and grabbed my shirt.

"Nothing!" he snapped. But he kept doing it, until he'd altered the rest of the shoes. Then he turned to me with a scowl. "Speak nothing of this." Then he gathered up the boxes and strode out toward the angry woman sitting in the midst of the tissue paper and empty box explosion. I peeked through the curtain.

"Madam. May I be of service?"

She unleashed a tirade of bluster that almost knocked his toupee off. But through it all, Meyer just nodded and smiled. When she took a breath, he moved in for the kill.

"Perhaps I should measure your foot . . . " Meyer cupped her Hobbit-like hoof in his hand as if he was cradling the Baby Jesus. "My, what lovely toes you have. That enamel, it's Persian Red?"

Her body language shifted instantly, her eyes widened, and her fists unclenched. Though she didn't know it, she'd just become another notch on Meyer's Brannock.

"Well . . . here's the problem. You're not a 10D, madam," sweet smile, "the Brannock reveals you are most definitely a 9B. No wonder those other shoes weren't flattering, they were inappropriately sized. I happen to have some 9B's right here. May I slip them onto those lovely feet?"

"I knew it," she sighed as he crammed the pump onto her sausage-width toes. She pranced in front of the mirror like a prom queen. "I'll take them all!" Quicker than I could say Coco Chanel, I was schlepping boxes to her car. When I returned, Meyer took me into the stock room and shut the door behind us.

"You must promise me you'll never speak of this. If any of these jackals learn that trick, they'll ruin us. They don't understand this business. All they care about is money, which is why they never have any. They don't understand that we're not selling shoes. We're selling the idea of shoes. Promise?"

"Yes. I promise."

He nodded sagely, pressed the two coins in my hand, and walked away. In that moment, I believed Meyer was the first

grownup I'd ever met smarter than me. Not only was he sending his customers away happy, but he was also booby-trapping every other salesman in Chicagoland. When the angry fat lady walks into another store and asks for a 9B, she's going to get even angrier. Eventually, like all his other clients, she'll only buy from Meyer, because he'll always give her more than shoes. Meyer gave his women the adoration they craved but would never ask for—someone who'll look at them like they're still young and radiant. He was right. I couldn't tell a soul. So I never did . . . uh, not counting the people who buy this book.

> **In that moment, I believed Meyer was the first grownup I'd ever met smarter than me. Not only was he sending his customers away happy, but he was also booby-trapping every other salesman in Chicagoland.**

Meyer was one of the first grownups I met that didn't treat me like a kid, even though I was. Our talks were always between equals, and looking back, I realize now that's one of the reasons I liked him so much. Some people just have that gift, that easy way of making you feel like you belong. Luckily, there are more Meyers in America. I just had to go looking for them.

One of the first I discovered sells pickles in a basement. You can go into any grocery store in the country and find aisles filled with jarred pickles, but that didn't stop Alan Kaufman from opening his own store—The Pickle Guy—on Manhattan's Lower East Side, to sell his own handmade kosher masterpieces. Like

COURTESY OF ALAN KAUFMAN/THE PICKLE GUYS

Meyer, he sold different models depending on the whims of his colorful clientele.

Bucking convenience, Alan dedicated his entire store to selling just pickled edibles. Pickles, olives, sauerkraut—anything that can be soaked in brine and sold by the pound, he's got. But that's all he's got. Try to buy a loaf of bread, some eggs, or a hammer and he'll heckle you back up to the sidewalk. It's just pickles, which means the people who come all the way down to the Lower East Side, knowing they can't do all their shopping in one place, must really love pickles . . . or Alan.

According to Alan, he's easy to love. Perpetually happy, Alan works the rough and tumble Lower East Side on Essex Street along a kosher strip of delis, tailors, and boarded buildings.

The Pickle Guy makes his sour magic in a walk-down bunker, filled with twenty open drums of different pickled treats.

The air is crisp and filled with the great smell of deli, "because you can't spell Delicious without Deli." Unlike most small shops in New York City, there are no point-of-purchase keno screens, cigarette cartons, or condoms for sale: no magazines, no lottery tickets, no energy drinks. But if you're looking for new, sour, or the elusive three-quarter pickles . . . jackpot!

I walked down off Essex Street and into a brick-lined room crammed with topless vats of pickled condiments and a small dry erase board scribbled full of prices to find the jovial Alan holding court. All around him, customers laughed and sampled his wares, while he snapped the pickles into tidbits. The brick kept the garlicky, vinegary smell from leaking out into the street, and provided great acoustics for the animated discussions that were raging in every corner of the store. The joint was jammed with authentic New Yorkers, and true to form, each of them had a loud opinion about something they were sure would interest you.

I like pickles as much as the next guy, but I'd never go out of my way to buy them at a special store. My shopping is much more efficient. I just dial up Cowboy Mouth or Buddy Guy on my iPod and float through a supermarket, filling my cart and tossing in some Vlasics along the way. Half an hour, tops, that's how guys shop. It took me longer than that just to cab it to The Pickle Guy, so who's got the time? Alan's regulars.

Ellen, the lady at the end of the line, rides in from Long Island. She was patiently waiting with six containers, ready to make her forty-five-minute trip back home. I asked her why she went through all the trouble. "These pickles are the best in the world."

Actually, I don't remember if she said "world" or "city," as if there's a difference with New Yorkers. But still, are even the

World's Greatest Pickles worth a two-hour train ride in a subway car with no AC and lots of shower-shunners? Why not save the time each week and just get them closer to home?

"Not the same," Ellen said while shaking her finger in my face. "These pickles have snap, they're crisp, and the garlic makes them delicious."

I struggled to squeeze past the zealots in line and found Alan in the back, stirring a vat of water with a kayak paddle. With just the twist of his wrist, he had the water zooming around the barrel like a vegetable Jacuzzi. There had to be a magic to his method, so I asked to see how he transformed ordinary vegetables into pickles with powerful pull over people from all five boroughs.

"First of all, you start with water," Alan intoned in a New Yorky voice perfectly suited for his occupation. "Then, ya add spices, kosher salt, and stir it up like a Jacuzzi. Then ya dump in a few cases of fresh cucumbers."

"Are they pickles yet?"

"Not yet, they are not pickles," Alan explained. Then he dumped in a bowl of vinegar. "Now they're pickles."

That's it. Cucumbers in brine, with whatever spices you like, are pickles. The artistry comes in the exact combination of spices, and how long you let them pickle, Alan's closely guarded secrets. He has a walk-in at the back of the store, filled with dated vats. When he empties one out front, he rolls out a new one.

"We make everything here," he says proudly as he muscles the newly minted pickles into the fridge. "That's why they're so good, no artificial preservatives, no chemicals. Just pickles. The longer they soak, the more . . . pickly they get."

"Whoa, whoa, whoa. Cut the jargon, give it to me in layman's terms."

He went on to explain that one to ten days makes a (virtually flavorless) "new pickle," and three months or more makes a lusty sour pickle. Alan sells mushrooms, olives, half and three-quarter pickles, and they're all delicious. But his bread and butter are the butter pickles.

But that's not why seventy-year-old Charles visits from Queens several times a week.

"I don't give a shit about pickles," Charles sneers. "Too much salt, my doctor won't let me. I'm here for my juice."

COURTESY OF ALAN KAUFMAN/THE PICKLE GUYS

Charles shouts out his order to Alan. "I want a container of juice. Sour, sauerkraut juice, to drink. That's what I want."

"He comes in every few days and wants to dip his own container into the sauerkraut vat to get the juice," Alan explains. "I keep telling him he can't, we gotta give him a new one to dip, but he always brings in his own. And we always throw it away. It's like a thing we got."

My Favorite . . . LUNCH

Four Seasons Hotel, Maui

The south side of beautiful Maui has been catering to lovers and strangers for years. Nestled twenty minutes from the best snorkel crater in the Islands, the Four Seasons is the old school tropical paradise that defines Maui luxury.

If you happen to be around on a Sunday, head to the restaurant for the best brunch you'll ever have.

Let's start with the view. The hotel is perched on an outcropping of land that sits high above the Pacific Ocean. The gentle crash of the waves and pulsing of the tide provide a soothing soundtrack for your meal. Cabanas abound and every square foot of outdoor space offers the best lunch spot in America.

Now to the food. Vegetables, meats, fruits—all of them are fresh and delicious. The bountiful varieties offered stun the senses. The buffet table looks like the scene from *A Christmas Carol* when the big, fat, loud ghost is showing Scrooge around. Opulent doesn't even begin to encompass it all.

Then there's the fish. Turns out, Maui is located in the middle of the ocean. The ocean is loaded with tuna, yellowtail, and all kinds of stuff just waiting to be turned into sashimi or fillets.

The Four Seasons gets them all, probably luring them to shore with the gorgeous grounds, then turns them into delicious, fresh, incredibly flavorful delights. If you love sushi, this will be a paradise. If you've never had sushi, don't start here, because then no matter where you try it next, it won't be as good.

No matter what you enjoy, you'll find it here in the sumptuous array of foods. Make a plate, find a spot, then try this fun experiment. Take a bite with your eyes closed. Savor the flavors. Then, take a bite with your mouth open . . . THEN you'll know why this is America's best lunch.

"I don't drink it regular. I mix it with tomato juice and make a cocktail." Charles describes his concoction to me with wild eyes: "It's a COCKTAIL! I drink it for vigor! Been doing it for years, and I never felt better. Try it!"

I do, and it's awful. Charles points out my twisted face to the rest of the patrons. His howls of laughter echo off the walls as I spit.

"Makes you pucker, huh? Ha ha ha!" Charles turns to the other picklers. "These kids, they don't know . . . but I know!"

They nod nervously, though I suspect they don't really know what Charles is ranting about. But there's no denying the zest and vitality with which he's doing it. Vampires achieve immortality by drinking blood, rich guys do it with trophy wives, evidently old Jews do it with a sauerkraut/tomato cocktail. Is that the Pickle Guy's secret recipe: everlasting life? If so, I'd add it to the sign.

> **Vampires achieve immortality by drinking blood, rich guys do it with trophy wives, evidently old Jews do it with a sauerkraut/tomato cocktail.**

Back in the day, any place people gathered, you'd find strangers talking. Maybe about the weather, maybe sports, always politics. Proximity and opportunity led to conversation. It's just the way things were. Before HD and LOL, talking was our main form of entertainment. People held conversations, they didn't send texts. Strangers listened while guys talked to their barbers and bankers.

But in the last few decades our rush to get connected has disconnected us. No one talks anymore. Is there anything we can do to fight back? Has the delicious enjoyment of just talking gone completely sour?

Sauerkraut, actually. I don't care how much Charles says he likes the puckering swill he concocts, he gets dressed, puts on his toupee, and schleps down to the Pickle Guy every few days . . . to shoot the shit. Drinking that crap is just the price he's willing to pay to indulge in the pleasure of random company. He loves being "the coot who drinks sauerkraut and tomato juice." He loves seeing the reaction on people's faces when he gets them to try his potion, and he loves laughing and chatting with all the other eccentric pickle gobblers that make the pilgrimage from their brightly lit, all-inclusive grocery stores to Alan's dank pickledrome. It's why they all come; the pickles are just their delicious excuse.

The kind of person who'll go out of their way for a particular pickle probably prefers people, pundits, and even random pedestrians to prolonged periods of protracted personal privatude. And after spending an afternoon in their shooting gallery, I realized that I needed some tonic, too.

I watched Alan working his register and noticed nobody was leaving. Patrons paid, then moved to the side to continue their

conversations. It was like the Pickle Hotel: customers checked in, but they didn't check out. And in the middle of it all, Ringmaster Alan smiled and kept the party going, offering samples, yelling jokes across the room, and calling customers by name. That's when I realized unassuming Alan, like Meyer Grumbakin before him, was a mastermind. Alan wasn't selling pickles—he was selling *the idea* of pickles. And once again, I was buying.

THE PICKLE GUYS PICKLE RECIPE

"We use number 2 kirbies and brine, which is salt water, then we add fresh cut garlic, and finally we add a mixture of pickling spices, which consists of coriander seeds, mustard seeds, dill seeds, dry pepper, some bay leaves.

"We pour it all into the barrels, then roll the barrels into our walk-in fridge. The amount of time they sit in the brine is how we determine what kind of pickles they are. New pickles are 1–10 days old, and taste like a salted cucumber. Half sours are 2–3 weeks old and are

COURTESY OF ALAN KAUFMAN/THE PICKLE GUYS

slightly sour. The full sour pickles are about 3 months old, they are the most pickled, sour, garlicky, and dill flavored. They are also the most popular pickle."

CHARLES'S SAUERKRAUT COCKTAIL RECIPE

1. Sneak into your neighborhood pickle store concealing an empty container. Make sure you also have its lid stashed somewhere on your person.
2. Have a friend create a disturbance across the room, then dip the container into an open sauerkraut vat and siphon off the acidic liquid. Affix the top and scurry home.
3. In the privacy of your own lair, mix sauerkraut juice with V-8 or tomato juice; add a little salt, pepper, and lime juice to taste.
4. Drink. Make funny face. Repeat.

COURTESY OF ALAN KAUFMAN/THE PICKLE GUYS

Chapter 9
Jazz Fest

In 1970 George Wein, the jazz impresario who created the Newport Jazz and Folk Festivals back in the 1950s, set out to create a small festival with a more diverse southern flavor. Forty years later, six hundred thousand people come through the gates for each New Orleans Jazz & Heritage Festival, because it's the best gastro-musical vacation in America. Period. If you enjoy live music, delicious food, and large, happy crowds, you must attend this sometimes muddy, always muggy bacchanal before your dirt nap. If you don't have fun in NOLA, call the papers 'cause you dead already.

New Orleans has everything a great city needs: uniquely delicious food, prepared by fervent locals who suck brain juice out of mudbugs—and do weird things too.

New Orleans is many menus that all happen to occupy the same crescent-shaped metropolis: FRIED: a Southern city, FRESH: a Mississippi river port, JERK: a gateway to the Caribbean, SAUCY: a historical hub for African and French immigrants. These disparate flavors blend with Bourbon Street's Dumpster funk to create an authenticity that faux-places like Times Square and all of Orlando can only envy.

Nouvelle Orleans was founded as a French colony in 1718, and from the beginning was filled with residents of "dubious" character. It spreads out along the Mississippi and boasts public squares and parks designed to actually be used by people! Its location as a port city attracted waves of riff-raff, deported slaves, gold hunters, and the used car salesmen of the day, fur trappers. They gravitated to the city for its lusty appetites and the Big Easy way culprits could quickly vanish into the bayou when the need arose.

But all them peoples got to eat. And from the get go, NOLA cuisine was a collaborative celebration blending the high art of French cooking with low-cost country game like alligator and catfish, drenched in Caribbean spices and served with traditional southern comfort foods. The catfish at a local Denny's is better than the "Cajun" restaurant in your town.

Memphis is ribs, Chicago is deep-dish pizza, and Maui is fish, the "best" of which depend only on who you happen to be talking to at the time. NOLA is gumbo. Each restaurant, every hotel, every greasy diner has their own recipe, and like a good potato chip, you can't eat just one. In New Orleans, even the gas stations are Zagat rated.

The Hotel Monteleone makes their gumbo from a thick, dark roux laced with okra. Commander's Palace has a redder, totally different gumbo that tastes somewhat like their turtle soup. But every gumbo shares a few essentials: the Holy Trinity—chopped celery, bell pepper, and onion—and the Pope, garlic. These savory veggies start out in a big pot with wheelbarrows of butter, flour, and spices. The resulting roux forms the stock for the meats each chef chooses to drop into their caldron, giving rise to endless bar fights all over town. Gumbo is a true melting pot, reflecting each chef's unique background and heritage. That's why you can eat gumbo 365 days a year, and twice on Mardi Gras, and never get bored.

Those same culinary currents also conspired to create America's most inventive musical scene. In the late 1800s the African influence from nearby plantations combined with colonial French-spawned folk music and merged with native southern and Caribbean rhythms. American jazz exploded in the 1920s and collided with voodoo, mojo, and gris gris, eventually creating Cajun, zydeco, and forming an unbroken second-line from Satchmo to the Nevilles. So when George Wein decided to produce a Jazz AND Heritage Festival, he knew it had to be as much about the food as the music.

But I didn't know any of that when my friends tried, yet again, to get me to join them for their annual Fest trip back in 1992. And really, I didn't care. I don't like crowds, overpriced, tasteless tent food, or waiting in long lines to whiz in a stinky plastic box. But when I learned that Albert King, Charles Brown, Al Green, Carole King, Blues Traveler, Marcia Ball, Dr. John, AND the Neville Brothers would all be playing . . . on one stage, over one weekend, I packed my bad attitude and got on the plane.

Fest was nothing like anything. I remember spending the first day in the middle of the racetrack infield, bopping along with fifty thousand people of every shape, smell, and color, sharing nothing but warm smiles and cold beer in the scorching sun, then coming back to the hotel to learn that Los Angeles was burning.

It was April 30th, the first day of the '92 L.A. riots. The contrast between here and there played out in black and white on my color TV. Strangers at Florence and Normandy were beating each other with bricks, while at the RayBan stage, they were harmonizing with "Amazing Grace."

Strangers at Florence and Normandy were beating each other with bricks, while at the RayBan stage, they were harmonizing with "Amazing Grace."

The next day, an uneasy calm blanketed the Fest. A few more police strolled the fairgrounds, and people were noticeably jittery. I couldn't sit still for long, and ended up walking to each of the nine stages to sample the performances. I was making my way back after a surprisingly brief foray to the not-horrific Porta-potty, when I heard some insane washboard playing. Buckwheat Zydeco was tearing up the Fais Do Do stage, so I stopped to listen. So did a large, sixty-year-old African woman. She was dressed in traditional garb that barely covered her shaking parts underneath. Our eyes met, and she stopped. I saw the news of the day flash over her face . . . can't even really explain what that means, except that in the twinkle of her eye, I saw fear, hate, shame, friendship . . .

then we danced. No words, just sweaty gyrations on a small patch of grass, adrift in a sea of people. The song went on for ten minutes, and we didn't stop. Buckwheat finally walked off the stage, leaving us panting. We hugged, then without saying a word, we each walked off. I've missed only one Fest since.

After fifteen Fests with the same group of friends, I attained Gris Gris status, which means I am qualified by the bylaws of our Bicoastal Bickering Board of Bastards to instruct mudbugs (newbies) in the ways of The Fest, based on the esoteric insights and drunken wisdom of our Board. I share these mystical secrets here in the hopes that your first Fest will be as fantastic as my last.

Jazz Fest always unfolds the last weekend in April and the first weekend in May. Six hundred bands perform on twelve stages scattered throughout the infield of the Fairgrounds Race Track just outside the French Quarter. It is too much festival to attend alone. You must go with a group of like-minded fun-seekers to maximize your enjoyment of this ninety-six-hour marathon. Carefully select your posse, because once you begin, you'll be seeing them for this weekend every year for the rest of your life. After fifteen-plus years, the B.B.B. of B has perfected the process of squeezing fun out of the bayou from sun-up to sun-up. But it ain't easy.

Agreeing which weekend to attend is the first hurdle; members exchange endless e-mails touting and dissing the competing musical lineups. Once the weekend is set, we all arrive in time to meet the night before at 6:00 p.m. at The Old Absinthe House on Bourbon Street for the first round. Pleasantries are exchanged, bourbon is consumed. The evening ends around midnight with much anticipation.

I always start my first Fest morning at Café du Monde, across from Jackson Square. Yes, it's crowded . . . and touristy . . . but it's worth it. Hack Bartholomew's trumpet caresses the thick morning air while the mysteriously all-Asian waitstaff takes their sweet time schlepping my chicory coffee and whole milk au laits and fried dough to my sticky table. On subsequent days, I go around back and stand in the "to-go" line—bigger cups, quicker service, but no Hack.

Once coffee is handled, it's time to head to the fairgrounds and establish base camp with the rest of the B.B.B. of B. Bands jam on scattered stages during the day, but someone always stays at base camp, usually established at one of the two main stages, where the members have laid out their chairs, blankets, coolers, and paraphernalia, based on the headliner we want to see at the end of the day. This allows members to explore the smaller acts, browse the craft booths, and never go more than thirty minutes without consuming something outrageously delicious. A group of six to twelve members is ideal, and ensures good seating and plentiful amenities. Members are especially useful for beer runs, food runs, and to fetch a medic when someone gets the runs from last night's Lucky Dog.

Lucky Dog

Lucky Dog \ luck-y dawg. \ [n.]. Edible [*sic*] hot dog sold exclusively on Bourbon Street, by straw-hatted carnies pushing red carts. Bourbon's unrivaled crush of drunken humanity provides a never-ending throng of late night revelers willing to eat almost anything . . . which is coincidentally exactly what goes into a Lucky Dog.

Festiquette dictates you never return to camp without sup-
plies: water, beers, food, something scrumptuous from one of
the six food areas spread across the fairgrounds. Sure, it adds
a few minutes to your humanity-clogged, comically serpentine
return, but it works. There's nothing better than waking from
a between-set nap to a surprise delivery of frozen Hurricanes
and fried chicken from a B.B.B. of B. delivery
angel.

Shows go on, rain
or shine. No matter what the Weather Channel says, how
sunny they promise it will be, bring rain gear . . . it's the bayou.
If you're lucky, it'll be 80 and humid; if you're not, it'll be an

aquarium. Buy chairs at the Walgreens in the Quarter across the street from the Monteleone, or buy the logo chairs and poncho/blanket combos at Fest so when you go to other festivals, people will know you played in the Bigs. I've used the same two green chairs since my first Fest. Every time I see an exceptionally brilliant set, I inscribe the artist's name on the fabric—like a favorite playlist. The chairs now contain a written record of my personal greatest hits, my version of Pyramid inscriptions.

Most music festivals in America are staged by greedy promoters, concerned only with squeezing every possible nickel out of you, while cramming you face-to-flanks with other suckers. They gouge you to get through the gate, then you're on your own. The sound stinks, the facilities are nonexistent, and the crappy, overpriced food is an afterthought at best, a midway of roach coaches that pay a ransom for the privilege of slopping their greasy glop to anyone starved enough not to care. Little or no thought is given to the overall experience of the fan; consequently you head home feeling like a backup prom date—dirty and used.

But not in New Orleans. Regardless of who's playing, everyone knows the food is always worth the trip. I stop eating the weekend before Fest. Just juice and vitamins until we touch down, then the world is my raw oyster. The world-class musical lineups are rivaled only by the cuisine, yes cuisine, available at strategically placed and fast-working booths around the infield. You will never eat a better assortment of delicious food anywhere in the world. Never. Nowhere.

All the authentic restaurants in town—and this is a foodie town—have booths at Fest and bring what they're famous for. Priced between $3 and $7, the portions are hot, portable, and

perfect. Unless you're an angry vegan, or a col-
legiate wrestler, it is impossible to leave Fest hungry. Write
this checklist on your hand and eat at least one of each, rain or
shine, before the music stops Sunday night:

    CRAWFISH SACK: Crawfish and sauce inside pastry. If Hot
        Pockets had a soul, and a thin, crispy pastry-like pouch
        in which to cradle fresh crawfish in a tangy sauce. Pat-
        ton's, Chalmette, Louisiana

    CRAWFISH MONICA: Creamy, orange sauce, thick with indi-
        vidual crawfish poured over fusilli pasta. Hot sauce
        mandatory, unless you want to incur the ridicule of the

hardcore eaters in line behind you. Kajun Kettle Foods, New Orleans, Louisiana

MINT-ROSE ICED TEA: When it's hot, it's heaven. Sunshine Concessions, Covington, Louisiana

GRILLED CHICKEN LIVERS W/ PEPPER JELLY, CROWDER PEAS AND OKRA: Robust, soul food for when you need more than gumbo to get your swamp fix. The Praline Connection, New Orleans, Louisiana

MUFFALETTA: Traditional round, meaty sandwich slathered with olive spread and topped with sesame seeds. Eat 'em hot. Napoleon's House, New Orleans, Louisiana

GUMBO: Pick three and have a foodie jam.

COUCHON D' LAIT PO'BOY: Perfectly seasoned bone-in pork roast. Twelve hours in the sizzling hickory pit yields succulent pulled pork that creator Wanda Boone Walker piles onto cool cabbage and the perfect French roll. Love at First Bite, New Orleans, Louisiana

BUCKET OF CRAWFISH: Suck the head and squeeze the tails. Any backyard barbecue in New Orleans, Louisiana

SOFT SHELL CRAB PO'BOY: Fried crab on French roll. Galley Seafood Restaurant, Metairie, Lousiana

CATFISH: Chef Duke's Blackened Cajun style. Café Giovanni, Decatur Street in the French Quarter

BOUDIN BALLS: Not an affliction, an addiction. Boudin blanc sausage chunks and rice rolled in egg and bread crumbs, then deep fried. Piggy popcorn from heaven. Papa Ninety Catering, Belle Chasse, Louisiana

JAMBALAYA: Like your tongue has won the lottery. Chunks of sausage, shrimp, Trinity with a dark, spicy sauce and plenty of rice. Unlike gumbo, you can pick up jambalaya with your hands and form into softball-size spheres. It would be pointless, but you could do it. Try it everywhere you go. No two are alike.

CRAWFISH ETOUFFEE: Mudbugs in zesty tomato-based roux, will not be found in your grocer's dairy case back home. Ledet & Louque, Gramercy, Louisiana

CRAWFISH BISQUE: Spicy, smooth, zesty. Like shrimp soup in a pink sauce . . . kinda. Lil Dizzy's Café, in a converted bank building located at 610 Poydras Street, New Orleans, Louisiana

CAFÉ AU LAIT: It's why people move here. Rich as Rockefeller, instantly tells you where you are and why you're there.

> **CRAWFISH SACK: Crawfish and sauce inside pastry. If Hot Pockets had a soul, and a thin, crispy pastry-like pouch in which to cradle fresh crawfish in a tangy sauce.**

At the beginning of the last encore around 6:40, fold up your blanket and pile your garbage into a neat pyramid for the volunteer clean-up crew before starting the slow weave back to the shuttle gate. Done correctly, the music will end just prior to boarding the coach for the crisp ride back home. This maneuver is known as the Alligator. Unlike most live events, the lines are reasonable and move quickly. If you were too dumb to buy the bus ticket, expect a sixty-minute wait in the cab line. Luckily, the line is patrolled by vendors selling barbecue, beer, and boudin. Cab lines don't get no better.

My Favorite . . . DINNER
Commander's Palace, New Orleans, Louisiana

Katrina really messed up the Commander. Water damage, wind, the place was a mess. The owners didn't let a little thing like the hurricane of the century slow them down. They simply closed down, remodeled, and opened up, better than ever.

COURTESY OF COMMANDER'S PALACE

Old school, elegant New Orleans dining has many expressions in the Crescent City. There are great neighborhood joints, many patio landmarks, and even the lunch counters on Decatur Street serve some of the best food in America. But if you've got a special occasion to celebrate, or a judge you want to bribe, there's only one place to get it done: Commander's Palace.

Located in the Garden District since 1880, this turquoise and white Victorian palace is the one location in a foodie city everyone can agree on.

The service is impeccable, the drinks outstanding, and the mojo palpable. Try the turtle soup, the fish, or the steaks. Nothing on the menu is less than jaw-droppingly incredible. A five-star restaurant in a ten-star city, walking out of Commander's Palace your feet don't touch ground again until you're back in the Quarter.

If you have only one elegant, extravagant multi-course meal the rest of your life, do it where Mark Twain enjoyed his.

After a taxi-meal like that, you'll want a shower and a nap . . . but make it quick, it's dinnertime. Reservations are a joke, it's Fest. If there's a member who owes a particularly large favor—for instance, if he urped on the communal blanket—drop them off at Mandina's on Canal on the way back to the Quarter, and when you deliver their change of clothes two hours later . . . your table will almost be ready.

Driving out of the Quarter for dinner will reduce your wait, but if you're on foot, there's plenty of great food right around the corner . . . but you'll wait for it. It's difficult, but not impossible, to have a bad meal in the Quarter. Since Katrina, due to the influx of Latin construction labor, several really good Mexican places have opened in the midst of the world-class Italian, French, and Cajun stalwarts that dot the Quarter. NOLA's list of bad restaurants is smaller than the junk in the trunk of a Hummer owner. For best results, use my DDS test. Walk the streets and stick your nose into every restaurant until you smell something too good to pass up. Then order a drink at the crowded bar, and pick a fight about who turned in the best set of the day. Time will fly.

> **Walk the streets and stick your nose into every restaurant until you smell something too good to pass up.**

On a good night, you'll be done with dinner at 11:00. Then it's music time again. Because the Fest draws world-class musicians, there's never a shortage of jammable talent in town. The larger clubs book several headliners a night, with showtimes at 10:00, midnight, and 2:00 a.m., making it possible to see an act scheduled to appear the

other weekend, or someone you missed during the day. Clubs like House of Blues, Tipitina's, Howlin' Wolf's, Maple Leaf, D.B.A., Carrollton Station, Mid City Rock 'n' Bowl, Le Bon Tempe Roule, and Mulate's present headliners in a barroom setting. The acts enjoy the intimacy of returning to their roots, and the patrons enjoy world-class music from chairs that don't collapse.

By 3:00 a.m. NOLA is getting its fifth wind, but you'll be done. Time to head home . . . via the grand Monteleone Hotel. This nineteenth-century landmark's majestic lobby and stylish rooms perfectly complement its main attraction, the world-famous Carousel Bar. This ornate circular bar was home to literary giants like Hemingway, Faulkner, and Tennessee Williams. Sadly, they're all dead and

My Favorite . . . HOTEL
Hotel Monteleone, 214 Rue Royal,
New Orleans, Louisiana

I've stayed in fancier hotels. I've stayed in schmancier hotels. I've stayed in places with better gyms, business centers, and big screens. But no hotel in America captures, preserves, and exudes the soul of its city more than the Monteleone— except maybe the filthy Ramada Plaza New Yorker Hotel, just a junkie's long-distance loogie from Madison Square Garden, and the only place I've ever slept wearing my clothes for fear of infection.

Nestled in the heart of the French Quarter, Antonio Monteleone's jewel has embodied Nawlin's hospitality and style since 1886. Whether you wake up in your room, or hunched over the almost imperceptibly rotating Carousel Bar, you instantly know exactly where you be. Have at least one drink at this lobby bar, where Tennessee Williams did some of his best work, and try to keep from laughing as clueless newbies return from the bathroom to find that their barstool— and friends—have mysteriously moved across the room.

The hotel is a short walk from Café du Monde in Jackson Square, Canal Street, and every dark, delicious dining room in the city. Be sure to take a late night walk up Bourbon to the Funky Pirate to catch Big Al Carson and the Blues Masters. The Monteleone is also just two blocks away from the best bar on Bourbon Street, the Old Absinthe Bar.

Built in 1807, the Absinthe manages to stay dark and dank, even though it sits on the corner of Bourbon and Bienville and features an entire wall of floor to ceiling French doors. Look around at the business cards on the wall. *Taste of America* was there . . . along with Mark Twain, P. T. Barnum, FDR, and Liza with a Z. Ridiculously salty popcorn is served . . . as if you needed a reason to drink here other than the inscription on the wall:

"Everyone you have known or ever will know, eventually ends up at the Old Absinthe House."

Yeah, you right.

COURTESY OF HOTEL MONTELEONE

not as scintillating as they used to be, so it's up to us to continue the tradition.

The best part of this legendary bar is the bar, a wooden circle that slowly revolves around the bartenders and their bottles. In fact it turns so slowly that many of the hotel's late-night revelers don't realize it's even moving. European tourists and buzzed First-Time Festers get off their stools and head to the bathroom, only to return and find someone else sitting in the seat they thought they left! One after the other, they stand in the doorway and puzzle, providing a nonstop parade of entertainment for anyone paying attention. Anguish flashes across their faces in the classic five stages:

Denial—That's my seat, get up!
Anger—Seriously Jagoff, THAT'S MY SEAT!
Bargaining—I'll buy you a drink if you give my seat back.
Depression—My friends bolted without saying goodnight.
Acceptance—Screw you, I'll sit somewhere else.

Which is right about the time the bar rotates back to reveal the seat they actually left and their guffawing friends. Watching this same scenario unfold three to ten times is the perfect nightcap to the most entertaining of days. Now you can go to sleep, then repeat the drill for the next three days. If you don't need a vacation, and an extended fast, upon your return home from the best music festival in America . . . you didn't do it right.

For those two weekends each and every year, don't make no difference who we are, what we do, or where we from . . . come hell or high water, we're all just part of NOLA's pungent gumbo.

COURTESY OF HOTEL MONTELEONE

CHEF RANDY BUCK'S
SEAFOOD AND FRIED OKRA GUMBO
Hotel Monteleone, New Orleans, Louisiana

3½ quarts fish stock

2 ounces chopped garlic

5 bay leaves

5 sprigs fresh thyme

2 cups dark brown roux, recipe follows

½ cup filé powder (seasoning made of sassafras leaves), dissolved in 1 cup water

¼ cup vegetable oil

1 large onion, diced

½ bunch celery, diced

2 green bell peppers, diced

2 Creole tomatoes, seeded and diced

¾ pound crawfish tails

1 pound medium shrimp

¾ pound backfin crabmeat

Salt and pepper to taste

Cayenne pepper

Fried okra, recipe follows

1. In a 2-gallon saucepot, combine fish stock, garlic, bay leaves, and thyme. Bring to a boil.
2. Add roux and allow to thicken. Reduce heat and simmer slowly.
3. Add dissolved filé powder and simmer for 1½ hours, skimming frequently.
4. In separate saucepot, heat oil over medium heat. Sauté onion, celery, peppers, and tomatoes until tender. Add seafood and cook for an additional 10 minutes, being careful not to overcook.
5. Transfer mixture to the gumbo base and simmer for another 10 minutes. Finish by adding salt, pepper, and cayenne pepper to taste. Ladle into bowls and top each with 3 or 4 pieces of fried okra.

Roux:

1 cup all-purpose flour

1 cup butter, melted

1. Preheat oven to 400°F.
2. Place flour into mixing bowl and pour butter in slowly, mixing until smooth.
3. Spread flour and butter mixture in a thin layer evenly in a shallow baking pan.
4. Bake for 45 minutes on center oven rack, stirring occasionally, until mixture turns a dark rich brown color.

Fried Okra:

½ cup vegetable oil for frying

3 eggs

1 cup water

1 cup all-purpose flour, seasoned with salt and pepper

2 cups Cajun corn flour

12 pods okra sliced into ½-inch pieces

1. Heat vegetable oil in pan or skillet until 350°F.
2. Combine eggs and water in a medium-size mixing bowl.
3. Place flour mixture and Cajun corn flour in two separate bowls.
4. Dredge okra in flour, then eggs, and then Cajun corn flour.
5. Carefully add okra to oil and deep fry for 5 minutes. Drain on a paper towel–lined plate.

COURTESY OF NAPOLEON HOUSE/SALVATORE I. IMPASTATO

MUFFALETTA RECIPE
Napoleon House Bar & Cafe, New Orleans, Louisiana
8-inch muffaletta bun with sesame seeds

4 slices ham (about 4 ounces)

5 slices Genoa salami (about 2½ ounces)

2 slices pastrami (about 1 ounce)

Italian Olive Salad spread evenly over surface

3 slices provolone cheese

3 slices Swiss cheese

1. Cut muffaletta bun open and layer with ingredients in this exact order.
2. Cut into 4 pieces and warm in microwave or oven till heated and flavors blend together.

Olive Salad Recipe

1 quart salad olives with pimiento—drained and sliced

6 ounces mixed vegetables—drained and chopped

6 ounces artichoke hearts—drained and chopped

6 ounces chickpeas—drained

6 ounces cocktail onions—drained

2 ounces capers—drained

2 ounces California pickled vegetables—drained and chopped

½ pound bell peppers—chopped

3 bunches celery—chopped

2 toes (or cloves) garlic—minced

1½ tablespoons oregano

1 cup olive oil

½ cup wine vinegar

Salt & pepper to taste

Mix everything together and let stand in fridge 24 hours so flavors will mix.

Makes ½ gallon

COMMANDER'S PALACE TURTLE SOUP

12 tablespoons (1½ sticks) butter

2½ pounds turtle meat (see note), cut in medium dice (beef, or a combination of lean beef and veal stew meat may be substituted)

Kosher salt and freshly ground pepper to taste

2 medium onions in medium dice

6 stalks celery in medium dice

1 large head garlic, cloves peeled and minced

3 bell peppers, any color, in medium dice

1 tablespoon ground dried thyme

1 tablespoon ground dried oregano

4 bay leaves

2 quarts veal stock

1 cup all-purpose flour

1 bottle (750 ml) dry sherry

1 tablespoon hot sauce or to taste

¼ cup Worcestershire sauce

2 large lemons, juiced

3 cups tomatoes, peeled, seeded, and coarsely chopped

10 ounces fresh spinach, washed thoroughly, stems removed, coarsely chopped

6 medium eggs, hard-boiled and chopped into large pieces

1. Melt 4 tablespoons of the butter in a large soup pot over medium to high heat. Brown the meat in the hot butter, season with salt and pepper, and cook for about 18 to 20 minutes, or until liquid is almost evaporated. Add the onions, celery, garlic, and peppers, stirring constantly, then add the thyme,

oregano, and bay leaves, and sauté for 20 to 25 minutes, until the vegetables have caramelized. Add the stock, bring to a boil, lower the heat, and simmer uncovered for 30 minutes, periodically skimming away any fat that comes to the top.

2. While the stock is simmering, make a roux in a separate pot: Melt the remaining 8 tablespoons of butter over medium heat in a small saucepan and add the flour a little at a time, stirring constantly with a wooden spoon. Be careful not to burn the roux. After all the flour has been added, cook for about 3 minutes until the roux smells nutty, is pale in color, and has the consistency of wet sand. Set aside until the soup is ready.

3. Using a whisk, vigorously stir the roux into the soup a little at a time to prevent lumping. Simmer for about 25 minutes. Stir to prevent sticking on the bottom.

4. Add the sherry, bring to a boil; add the hot sauce and the Worcestershire, and simmer, skimming any fat or foam that comes to the top. Add the lemon juice and tomatoes, and return to a simmer. Add the spinach and the chopped egg, bring to a simmer, and adjust salt and pepper as needed.

Note: We use alligator snapping turtles, a farm-raised, freshwater species available all year. It's illegal to use sea-raised turtle, so farm-raised is fine. Turtle meat usually comes in 2½-pound portions, so this recipe is written to use that quantity. It freezes well and can be ordered by mail.

Serves 12–14

NEW ORLEANS CAFÉ AU LAIT

Mix equal parts French Market Coffee with hot whole milk. Serve in a mug on a sticky table with sugar to taste. That delicious, nutty taste is chicory, courtesy of monks from the 1600s. They, and the Dutch who were responsible for shipping chicory-laced coffee all over the world, believed it gave the drink superior color, flavor, and body. It also reduced the amount of coffee beans needed, boosting profit margins. Think of that the next time an Internet coffee date wants to "go Dutch."

Chapter 10
Bachelor Party BOOFTAR

When I'm not traveling for work, it's nice to go someplace just for fun. But even on leisure trips, I approach the planning and execution with the same bag of tools, which is why my friends keep my number in their favorites—eventually, like a dentist or an undertaker, I am needed.

Because there comes a point in every life when it's time to put away childish things. Usually, it's the weekend before your wedding. Since college, whenever the need arose to break from the daily routine and convene someplace other than home, it fell to me to construct a weekend of harmless debauchery. Because of this innate talent and practiced skill, I have become known as . . . Captain Fun, Bachelor Party Booftar. I am the Booftar because I know The Secret: the Key to any and all successful group excursions is GOOD FOOD. If people are well fed, nothing else matters.

If I've been where we're going before, I call a few friends and get my update. I don't trust all the Web "review" sites. One review is horribly bitter, the next sounds like it was written by the owner. I go to the source. If I haven't been there before, I call a concierge or the local chamber of commerce—during lunch hour so I can talk to the assistants. They always run the show, and are usually more willing to share the good AND the bad/ugly. I pick their brains about shows, attractions, and locations that shouldn't be missed. When should we visit? Are there seasonal festivals, is there a show or event that brings out the best of the city? In travel, as in love and pie throwing, timing is everything.

> **In travel, as in love and pie throwing, timing is everything.**

Next, I pick my top three hotels and call into the restaurant or bell desks to find out from the staff where they eat. As we have learned, the hospitality cabal is the ultimate source for quality food and great locations. By compiling my guy-tinerary before leaving home, I'm ready to push, prod, and move the group like kids on a field trip. There's nothing worse than a bunch of guys waiting around a hotel lobby, texting and watching each other's hair gel harden. Effortlessly delivering your gang to a great restaurant or club time after time is how you earn "Booftar" status. It also buys some goodwill in case other events during the weekend tank.

NEVER allow guys to stay at different hotels—the logistics alone will drive you to drink, and not in a good way. Take cabs—but don't be an idiot. Have a general idea of where you're going so if some sleazy cabbie takes you the long way, you can enjoy the delicious thrill of explaining to him exactly where he screwed you, while paying him half his fattened-up fare. If he gives you any crap, take his picture and one of his licenses; it will immediately shut him down, even though I have no idea whom you would send it to.

When I'm booking a block of rooms, I've got the power. I always include the food and beverage manager in the negotiations. If you have a big enough group, you can negotiate a

flat rate for breakfast vouchers or discounts
on drinks. The main goal of the bachelor party is to create camaraderie between the different sects of the bachelor's life,
and communal coffee and morning storytime is a good start.
The feat is completed via the stomach.

Guys know, but women don't believe, that like all good parties,
even bachelor bashes revolve around food. Liquor and lovelies
play their parts, but to turn a disconnected rabble into a cohesive,
fighting unit, pull their pallets around a table with a quickly orbit-
ing waitstaff and you've created a team of world-class wingmen.

Of all my bachelor party successes, the *fete de tutti fete* was my
brother Dan's party. He was young and most of his pals didn't have

deep pockets, so we needed a destination that was affordable yet flexible. The wedding was scheduled for Los Angeles, so Vegas was the obvious choice. But obvious doesn't have to mean ordinary.

Las Vegas, like America itself, is more than one destination, just like the Rio Resort and Casino's Carnival World Buffet. There, you can go everywhere without even changing forks. In the real world, you have to change your underwear—at least— while getting from China to Italy. On the Strip, you have to drive from geographically themed restaurant to geographically themed restaurant. And it takes over an hour to walk from the New York Deli at New York, New York to the New York Deli at Bally's. But at the Rio, you can go from China to Italy in nine steps. They never lose your luggage, and it's more than authentic enough for a bachelor party.

> **In the real world, you have to change your underwear —at least—while getting from China to Italy. On the Strip, you have to drive from geographically themed restaurant to geographically themed restaurant.**

I made Dan's Wednesday to Friday jaunt all-inclusive. Guys sent checks upfront to prepay hotel and activities, getting us better mid-week rates, and making everyone feel like high-rollers because everything looked comped. Attitude is very important, especially in Vegas. Wear hats, walk with a swagger, and never let 'em know you're playing at the nickel slots.

Our group of eighteen convened in a remote Los Angeles parking lot early Wednesday morning. I'd rented an RV and

stocked it with Jack Daniel's, Corona, videos (some naughty, some nice), and ribeyes. The RV had a mobile grill so we charred our way down I-10. While other travelers stopped in Baker to see the giant thermometer and choke down dry pie, we sailed on, leaving a delicious smokey billow in our wake. Steaks, corn, double-baked potatoes, and all the fixins made the six-hour trip feel like a fancy steakhouse dinner, without the creamed spinach.

While we were away, the bride was having her bachelorette party, and was miffed Dan wouldn't be there to meet her out-of-town friends until the day before the wedding.

BRIDES: here's a warning sign. Any guy who says he really wants to attend your femme fest is either a liar or spineless. Either way, bad husband material. Conversely, any guy who adamantly refuses to attend is exactly the kind of guy you want to attend, because all your girlfriends will love him. Catch-22. But don't fret, you'll have plenty of years to twist your fiancé into the perfect husband. As we know, men are easy: shiny objects, a flash of lace, and something delicious, and we'll follow you anywhere.

Upon check-in we went immediately to the pool to wait for guys coming in from other cities. As they showed up, they were required to buy a round and tell one embarrassing story about someone in the group. To ensure we heard some quality dirt, the best story earned its author $50 in casino chips. I will not recount the winning story here, but I will offer this insight: Before leaving a Las Vegas bar/club with a new female friend, make sure you perform the Adam's apple test in adequate lighting.

Especially in Vegas, a group's first meal should always be a buffet. Take a stroll past the entrees before you get in line—there's always a line—and evaluate the stations that set the bar: king crab, prime rib, salad bar. You're looking for obscene quantity, because in Vegas "more" is classier than "good." The Bellagio, the Wynn, and the Venetian stand out because they offer both. The bowls of king crab legs at the Bellagio are large enough to baptize babies in—old school, totally under water, fire and brimstone baptisms. Chef Wolfgang Von Wieser makes the entrees run on time, keeping everything piping hot, fresh, and un-buffety. The carving station at the Wynn has its own security. Zeffirno, the Venetian's Sunday buffet, marries Italian opulence and American gluttony into a palatable zuppe. The only thing you miss by patronizing these top-tier buffets, rather than the "value-priced" feed troughs around town that mysteriously paint their walls purple and make their chairs plastic, is the Wal-Mart fashion show. Sitting at those places while curiously clad, fanny-packed Americans waddle through the line for the FIFTH time really makes you feel good about your own fashion sense. If you didn't chuckle at the previous sentence, visit www .peopleofwalmart.com and pray you don't see yourself.

After-dinner is all about gaming, drinking, and bonding. Lots of Dan's friends had heard about each other, but never met. It was hilarious to put faces to the famous stories and hear the friend's side of the story. Guys raged deep into the night, fortunes were won and lost—the rest stays in Vegas.

Thursday before noon we all piled into the RV and drove off the strip to Flyaway indoor skydiving. Their converted warehouse houses a 707 jet engine inside a giant tube. Guys strap into flight suits, then leap into the jet-wash for indoor simulated skydiving. It's just like real skydiving, except you really have to try to die while doing it. Mostly, you just get tossed around like a popping corn kernel, bouncing off the walls and momentarily floating in midair. Thus the pre-lunch schedule.

After two hours of flying/crashing into each other, it was finally time to eat, so on the way home we stopped at the Las Vegas Club and ordered their nine-pound hamburger. To honor the city and its fans, the Las Vegas Club bakes up a fat slab of meat resting on two oversized buns.

Stunt food is perfect for bachelor parties. Really, only for bachelor parties. When else would you order a nine-pound burger with all the fixins? The problem is something so large is hard to cook—the middle's too red and the outside is burnt to a crisp. Yet, the spectacle of the food being delivered by six girls in outfits that make Hooters girls look like debutantes made everything all right. That burger, and the beers that washed it down, proved to be the perfect snack before returning to the pool to ogle bachelorette parties and sweat out toxins while mulling our dinner destination.

Every chef who can boil water has hung out his apron on the Strip in the last decade. Exotic food and exquisite ambience is available everywhere—but with a group of young dudes, I was constrained by price and style. It's overkill to inject twenty-five guys into the Cantonese opulence of the MGM's Pearl without dates to dazzle. Did we really need the nine thousand–bottle wine tower at Aureole in Mandalay Bay after guzzling Old Milwaukee Light all day around the pool? The guys voted Italian, but Il Mulino in Caesar's Forum Shops—a great place for northern Italian cuisine—couldn't accommodate a group of twenty-five on two hours notice. I offered a list of nine other places the local gastro-gang hipped me to, but each one was out of reach in some way. At 5:00 p.m. I was facing a potential meltdown on our last night in town, not very Booftar of me. I looked at the circus unfolding in front of me at the pool and saw my savior. He was

My Favorite . . . GREASY DELIGHT
Al's Beef, Chicago

There's a reason all Chicago Bears fans have the same large, soft, pear-shaped body: Al's Beef.

There are several Al's sandwich shops scattered throughout the Chicagoland area, but the original one on Taylor Street is the place where it all started.

Winter or summer, day or night, your trip to Chicago is not complete until you have an Italian beef sangwich.

Italian beefs are greasy, bulky heart attacks wrapped in wax paper. The beef is slow cooked with Al's secret blend of herbs and spices for hours before the chefs pull out the slab and slice it paper thin. Then, they take the mounds of beef and soak them in their own juice for hours until you order one.

When you do, they split a homemade baked French roll, dunk it open-faced in the juice, then pile on a pound of the meat.

Then they ask "Sweet or hot?" They're not referring to how you like your prom dates, they're asking about peppers. Sweet green peppers to layer onto the meat, or spicy and very,

very hot Giardinera peppers—a chopped mix of vegetables soaked in peppery oil—yes, more oil—to scoop onto the meat.

They add the peppers, wrap it all up in paper that gets transparent the moment it touches the greasy bread, and hand it to you over the counter.

They're about $10 for a full size and worth every penny.

DO NOT EAT THIS IN YOUR CAR.

It is not possible to eat a Beef in your car unless you are naked. And if you are, why are you having lunch? The only place to safely eat a Beef is at the counter, while twisted into the Beef Lean—the only thing lean about this meal.

Unwrap the sangwich and place it in front of you on the high counter.

Roll up your sleeves and place your elbows on the counter.

Push your ass five steps back, without moving your elbows, causing your entire body to lean away from the counter, thereby clearing a nice drop zone between your mouth and the floor so as not to drip or drop beef, juice, or peppers on your nice shirt, pants, or shoes. And by "nice shirt," I mean either a Payton, Butkus, or Urlacher Bears jersey.

Now take a bite and introduce your mouth to nirvana.

Note: Beefs do not keep well overnight. They do not make good leftovers. You've got to eat them fresh and hot, ideally while talking sports to other leaning lovers around you. If you eat more than one of these a week, you're going to need an entire new wardrobe of loose-fitting Blackhawks jerseys.

one hundred yards away, perched above the fray on his lifeguard chair, serenely watching all the mini-dramas playing out beneath him. I knew in my gut, he'd steer me to the promised land.

Tony had been the head lifeguard for a long time. At fifty-nine, he could still "kick anyone's ass" and looked sharp, tanned, and crammed into his red Speedo. Some guys can just pull it off. The tufts of gray chest hair against his Rawlings-brown skin provided the perfect pillow for his entire gold chain collection, which was evidently too valuable to leave in a vault and needed to be kept on his person at all times. When he told me he was an Italian guy from New Jersey, I pretended to be surprised.

"Don't patronize me, asshole. I'm trying to help you out here," he smirked. "You want good, family-style food I'll send you to the place. They'll take your friends and treat them like kings. Tell 'em Tony at the Pool sent ya."

With no other viable options, I sheepishly called the place and told them twenty-five guys wanted to eat at 7:30. The host laughed, no way. We could put our names on the list, and wait . . . probably ninety minutes. Time to toss up my Hail Mary.

"Tony at the pool told me to call." Silence.

"Something just opened up sir. We'll be happy to seat your party at 7:45. *Buon pomeriggio.*" ("Good afternoon" for those of you who aren't Italian guys from New Jersey.)

And so it was that we cleaned up and headed off the Strip to a small Italian place that should be the Wikipedia entry for "Italian joint" in Vegas.

There are two kinds of Italian restaurants in America—fine establishments with linen napkins and long wine lists to be patronized when impressing a date or client, and joints that formerly harbored Rat Pack wannabes, their "exotic dancer" consorts, alongside members of law enforcement. Clearly, Tony was not trying to impress anyone.

Battista's has been family owned and operated from the same mini-mall for over thirty years. Scenically located between a tacky grocery store and grimy all-night liquor store, overlooking the picturesque Bally's parking structure, "Battista's Hole in the Wall" is the hole to which all other holes should aspire.

We blustered into the joint, twenty-five strong, and were led to our private room. The fixed-price menu includes more than you can eat: classic minestrone or salad, pasta side, garlic bread, and heavy, red sauce entrees . . . plus all the house wine you can drink. The waitresses are relics of Vegas's heyday. The garlic bread arrives in red plastic baskets through dark, wood-covered rooms sprawling in all directions. Tony turned out to be our lifesaver.

But our brother was getting hitched; we needed more than freebie, though drinkable, house wine. Luckily, Brother Mike the oenophile brought a case of imported wine from home,

> **There are two kinds of Italian restaurants in America—fine establishments with linen napkins and long wine lists to be patronized when impressing a date or client, and joints that formerly harbored Rat Pack wannabes, their "exotic dancer" consorts, alongside members of law enforcement.**

so rather than ordering good wine for $100 a bottle, we drank spectacular wine for $50 a bottle. In Vegas slip your waiter a Chicago Fiddy and you won't even pay the corkage fee.

Within moments of our Battista's arrival, we'd attracted the attention of Gordy, the wandering accordion player. Gordy's forte is playing a song based on your hometown. You know you're in Battista's when you're hearing "I Love L.A.!" on the squeeze-box.

Battista's has survived Vegas this long because they understand what their demographics want: large portions of classic entrees slathered in red sauce, garlic bread soaked in butter, and palatable seafood in the middle of a desert. Most important, Battista's avoids the snobby patina many of the newer, chef-centric egodromes exude, though the heavy stench of Aqua Velva and Barbisol does take some getting used to.

A Chicago Fiddy

A Chicago Fiddy is a carefully folded $50 bill, $50 showing, stashed in the palm. The subject is approached with palms upturned, and a hushed conversation ensues wherein you ask for his/her help. At the conclusion of the conversation, you grab his/her right hand with your left hand and guide him/her into a handshake wherein the bill is transferred to the subject. Thank him/her sincerely and walk away. Ninety percent of the time, you will receive your favor. For the other 10 percent, you are free to verbally chastise the server for the rest of the evening, as long as your remarks are funny. If you get snotty, you look like a jagoff.

We ate and drank and reveled to our own municipal soundtracks until "the itch" spread through the room. Somewhere close, dice were rolling, cards were snapping, and wheels were spinning without us. And that was not right. We paid the check from the communal account, slipped some cash into Gordy's cummerbund, and raced out to meet the night.

Showtime! In Vegas, it can be a cheesy production show with showgirls, a crappy comic and some juggling, a concert at the House of Blues, an X-rated hypnotist, or one of the eleven Cirque du Soleil shows in town. A month out, I'd sent the guys a query with three show choices, all of which featured audience participation. Dan ended up getting pulled onto the Riviera stage by two six-foot-tall showgirls and doused with a fire extinguisher. Totally Booftar.

    But at some point, even the best
party planner has to let his vultures leave the nest. Clubbers
peel off, gamblers shake it, and guys on the make . . . do both.
The group fractures all over town, and details don't emerge until
. . . the morning after.

    Coffee on Friday morning was slower, and later than Thurs-
day's edition. Until Strange Johnny (we all had nicknames now)
stumbled to the table, screaming into his cellphone.

    The bank was on the other end, explaining to him that his
entire checking account had been drained last night. Johnny
insisted that wasn't possible because his debit card had never left
his wallet, except when he gave it to his new friend, Krystal the

Dancer, when they stopped to buy Jagermeister on the way back to the hotel last night. She was nice enough to let Johnny wait in the cab, a traditional "you buy, I'll fly" arrangement, and gave it back when she returned. At that point, it sounded to us like the bank wanted to talk to Krystal, but Johnny had to explain that she'd left early, sweetly allowing him to sleep. He'd tried her cell, but she probably turned it off while she was in class. At that point the bank must have said something uncomplimentary about Krystal, because Johnny cursed them out and hung up.

He plopped himself down in the middle of our hushed table of fifteen (VERY important to have breakfast vouchers— ensures everyone hears all the good stories fresh and firsthand), and looked like he was going to weep into Dan's frittata.

"She is an angel," he sobbed. "From the moment we met, we didn't leave the VIP room . . . until her shift ended. Magic. I looked deep into her eyes and I saw our future. She saw it too. There's no way she did this. She's a goddess. Smart, classy . . . and double-jointed. Look at these."

Looks of stunned admiration, abject disgust, and jealous incredulity followed Johnny's photo-laden iPhone as it made its way around the table to me. When the smartphone finally arrived next to my pancakes, my face joined the gallery. Unless she's being taught by nuns, this girl is earning straight A's. I asked Johnny how much she stole.

"Everything. $4,300. All of it. Online gift cards. What kind of bullshit Web site sells four grand in gift cards at 5:17 through 5:23 a.m.?!"

We did our best to calm Johnny down, coaxing him back onto the RV with pork rinds and breakfast Cuervo. Because that's what wingmen do.

Our noon head count somehow turned out correct, so the RV pulled onto I-15 on time and we headed back to real life. Noticeably quieter on the way back, the rest of the stories didn't start to gurgle until the sun sank behind the mountains. That's when we found out Gary won $5,000 at the bar on video poker, while being hit on by no less than three transsexual prostitutes, then lost $6,000 on a three-game parlay. Jimbo threw up on security after riding down the main staircase in a garbage can. And a mystery was solved when Dave and Dave confessed to dumping ice into the beds of the guys who ditched them before heading to Cheetas. For revenge, the Daves soap-scrawled "No money to gamble, too much time to think" on the bathroom mirror of the offenders. By the time we reached Barstow, their soapy slogan had been transformed into a fully orchestrated rock anthem. It was eventually recorded by the local LA band Hempstead Nursery as "Vegas, Vegas, Vegas." To this day, no one can speak of that weekend without at least humming the infectious chorus.

It was dark by the time we got back home. Guys, who only fifty hours before had been total strangers, mumbled heartfelt Bro-Byes, slumped into their cars, and reluctantly drove away. But for those with lovelies waiting for them at home, the night was far from over. The most difficult part of the bachelor party was still ahead: walking through the front door and passing The Quiz.

What Significant Others fail to realize is that vague answers and lack of detail are not deceptions, but vestiges of sleep deprivation and early-onset detox trauma.

The facts, figures, and phone numbers from the weekend aren't the story. Skirts aren't chased as much as discussed, dissected, and appreciated from afar: at least by the attached guys. So that by the time you drag yourself back home, though you'd never say it out loud on the RV, the most glorious sight of the weekend is the groggy one that greets you from your own rumpled bed.

To steal from the best, it's a weekend about nothing. And if each attendee comes home with a mind full of memories too nuanced, or stupid, to adequately explain to their beloved, the best man earned his tux. If not . . . you should've called me.

> **What Significant Others fail to realize is that vague answers and lack of detail are not deceptions, but vestiges of sleep deprivation and early-onset detox trauma.**

Ultimately, a bachelor party is like the air inside a car—people only talk about it when it stinks.

BACHELOR PARTY: SERVES UP TO TWENTY-FIVE

Rent large mode of conveyance, add cliques of friends. Drive loudly away from home toward location with much visual, auditory, and gastronomical stimulation. Mix thoroughly.

EAT. Eat. Eat. A good army travels on its stomach. A good party is too full to travel anywhere . . . but the buffet.

Add group activities, food, liquor, entertainment, and a Kafka-esque assortment of strangers. Mix more thoroughly. Confiscate cameras (but keep yours). Stay safe and sane . . . but juuuust barely. Talk to strangers, hug your friends, and irritate the right people.

Return home and when asked, always begin your stories with a chuckle.

Chapter 11
Meat Heads

I've lived most of my life in two big cities, Chicago then Los Angeles. In between I went to college in Des Moines, Iowa, though I can't explain why. Ironically, the cornbelt coma that smothered me freshman year forced me to seek entertainment off campus, so I started doing comedy in a converted soup kitchen. I was making $100 a weekend telling jokes to farmers, while dating their daughters during the week. The night I won an award in the annual campus variety show, I realized it didn't matter what major I wrote down on my paperwork, I was going to be an entertainer. If I could make it in Des Moines, I could make it anywhere!

The big party night in Des Moines was Wednesday: quarter drafts at Peggy's. Cheap beer and a night of cow tipping was a great way to kill an evening, but after two semesters, I needed a city with a pulse. The day I finalized my transfer to UCLA, Mike Havice, the head of the Radio/TV Department—at a university without either a radio or TV station—sat me down in his basement office, looked sternly across his desk, and gave me the gift of his wisdom.

"You'll be back, DeCarlo," he said as the fluorescent light flickered over his graying hair. "They all come back from L.A."

And he was right; it was only twenty years later that I found myself in Pioneer Park, the AAA home of the Iowa Cubs, devouring Maid-Rite sandwiches and drilling baseballs into the parking lot beyond left field, as pitchers from the state champion high school team tried to whiff me.

Iowans are very proud of their high school sports and their Maid-Rite sandwich because, let's face it, besides the University of Iowa's Writers' Workshop and the *Better Homes and Gardens* Test Garden, Iowa doesn't make a lot of top ten lists.

The Maid-Rite was "invented" in 1926 in Muscatine, Iowa, when Fred Angell, a local butcher, took scraps from his shop, ground 'em up special, and seasoned them just right. He put the loose meat on a fresh, warm bun and by virtue of his wife's marketing genius birthed a franchising dynasty. The sandwiches are delicious—just ask anyone in Des Moines—but are they revolutionary? No. In fact, they're one of the most obvious food inventions I've ever eaten. The only difference, really, between a Maid-Rite and a hamburger is shape.

Yet Maid-Rite enjoys a fanatical devotion among Iowans. People gush about their first Maid-Rite, or how far they drove to get a sandwich, or why it's different than a sloppy joe (the sauce). One grandmother actually got teary-eyed describing her first visit with her grandchild.

"But it's just a Manwich," I teased her. "What's the big deal? It's a poorly made hamburger."

"No, no it's not," she sniffled. "It's our sandwich. I'm proud of our sandwich."

Proud . . . of a sandwich? If you'd invented it yourself, maybe. If you're NOLA's Central Grocery, and you'd perfected the mix of deli meats, olive spread, and cheeses on round, toasted sesame bread and called it the Muffaletta, yeah be proud. Or if you were the first guy to realize that adding bacon to anything makes it better, sure, pat yourself on the back and leave a greasy stain on your shirt. But pride in a broken burger just because it was invented in your area code? That's not about the food, that's ego.

It gets better. When I contacted Maid-Rite to get some tasty pictures of their sandwich and their recipe for this book, my call was shunted to a chirpy PR drone who was devastated to inform me that "we don't give out our recipe."

"But . . . it's just crumbled hamburger meat. I could write that recipe on the back of a snowflake," I demurred. "You're seriously going to refuse to divulge the array of spices that I could find reading the back of a Manwich can?"

"That's our policy."

I get it. If I publish their recipe, then any idiot could make 'em rite at home, which means the terrorists win.

"Can you send me a photo so that I can give your business some free publicity and celebrate your Midwestern heritage?"

Check the end of this chapter for the answer to that one.

Luckily, Mad Dog and Merrill, two DJ/chefs also from the Midwest, enthusiastically shared with me their recipe for "The Ultimate Burger." Seven different hamburgers stacked on top of each other—like an entire burger buffet on one skewer.

Unfortunately, their recipe was nowhere near as complicated as a broken hamburger—he typed sarcastically. Mad Dog and Merrill were only too happy to detail the intricate details of how to cook and assemble seven, yes seven, different types of burgers into one, gigantic burger-skewer and even how to eat it without perishing. By combining all the different tastes of backyard barbecue burgers into one monster, everyone gets what they want . . . unless you want crumbled meat with mystery seasonings.

But I don't blame Maid-Rite for being hostile to me. After all, I live in a big city . . . and we're at war!

I've discovered that in addition to all our other problems, America is enduring an escalating culture clash between Small Town and Big City. It's the reason everyone hates New York . . . well, one of the reasons. It's why when a rock band sings the name of your city in a song, you scream. There are many expressions of our complex Big City vs. Small Town syndrome, but the yin and yang ultimately boils down to parking: If you never worry about finding a space, you're in a small town. If you do, you're in a big city. If you're still not sure which kind of metropolis you live in, take this simple quiz:

1. For one million dollars, what's the full name of the person living across the street from you? $250,000 for just the first name? Is your mail carrier male or female?
2. Can you fly to a vacation destination without changing planes?
3. When you get pulled over by the cops, are you more concerned about the ticket or what the cop will tell your parents?
4. Have you ever been seen on TV in the crowd of a local sporting event?
5. When you tell friends you're traveling to New York City do they fear for your life or tell you to say "Hi" to Regis?
6. Have you ever eaten an animal you named and raised?
7. Regardless of the year, did more than 20 percent of the guys in your senior class photo wear mullets?

If you answered "A" to more than three questions, you were taking the wrong quiz.

Iowans aren't the only offenders. In Seymour, Wisconsin, local high school coach Bill Collar proves Seymour's superiority every weekend by costuming himself as the closest thing meat has to a superhero: Hamburger Charlie.

> There are many expressions of our complex Big City vs. Small Town syndrome, but the yin and yang ultimately boils down to parking: If you never worry about finding a space, you're in a small town.

According to Bill, and anyone else in town you might ask, the hamburger was invented in Seymour, Wisconsin, in 1885 when fifteen-year-old Charlie Nagreen decided to sell hot meatballs at the town's first annual fair. Once he and his ox-drawn cart got to the fair, Charlie realized that no one wanted to sit down and eat meatballs; they wanted to walk around and see the prize cattle, sheep, and farm machinery. They needed a portable food, so Charlie took two pieces of bread and flattened his meatballs between them. He named his invention the "hamburger" because of the large German immigrant population in the area—thinking they'd sell

COURTESY OF BRIAN MILLER

if named for something familiar, and because there was already a food named Bismarck.

Overnight, he became "Hamburger" Charlie, and Seymour proudly christened itself, "The Home of the Hamburger." You might think any guy who'd sacrifice his weekends to dress up like a dead short order cook and recite a memorized 508-word poem about meat is nuts. I certainly did, especially when the first thing Bill Collar wanted to do when we met was show me around a museum dedicated to hamburgers. But I was wrong.

WWW.HOMEOFTHEHAMBURGER.ORG

The Hamburger Museum is housed in a converted storefront next to the park where the statue of Hamburger Charlie stands vigil over hungry pigeons and week-

> You might think any guy who'd sacrifice his week-ends to dress up like a dead short order cook and recite a memorized 508-word poem about meat is nuts.

end barbecues. Through donations and volunteer labor, the town stuffed the small, brick building with every meaty artifact they could find. There are old photos of the real Hamburger Charlie (a dead ringer for Bill), newspaper articles Bill painstakingly reads aloud establishing 1885 as the year, and Seymour as the place, where the hamburger was born, as well as vintage McDonald's and Burger King toys, slogans, and hats, all without a whiff of postmodern irony. It's Bill's Library of Congress; for the rest of us, it's the Taj Mahal with cheese—an intoxicating mixture of cache and kitsch that comes complete with its own short-order concierge.

Unlike a lot of other "mascots" I meet on the road, Bill is not a crazy, delusional huckster. He has no evil, ulterior motive for dressing up in all white and giving away very delicious hamburgers fried in

COURTESY OF BRIAN MILLER

My Favorite . . . STEAK
The Fort Restaurant, 19191 Highway 8,
Morrison, Colorado

The Fort is located on the southwest outskirts of Denver, with Rocky Mountain views to forever. It's a frontier restaurant, complete with gift shop and Native Reenactments. But that's not why you go. Neither are the Rocky Mountain oysters . . . but if you've lost a bet, they're an option.

You go hungry and you go for "Scout Jim Baker's Mountain Man Steak." This twenty-ounce bone-in ribeye of Buffalo meat is more tender and tasty than beef, and lower in cholesterol too. Because the buffalo are free-range, locally grown livestock, the meat is healthier, especially when you sit down and eat a pound and a quarter of it. Regardless, the buffalo ribeye makes for the most delicious, mouth-watering steak I've had. Make a night of it, because it's a drive. But if you like food—and who doesn't these days—it's worth the trip. At least you're not stuck doing it in a covered wagon.

butter. He's not even Hamburger Charlie all the time. Most of the time he teaches science and coaches sports at the local high school. And I bet he's a great coach, tough, fair, and with just enough whimsy to keep the kids focused and motivated.

Bill is committed to convincing the world that Seymour is Grill Zero. In addition to appearing at local games and events, he also gives tours of the museum whenever people happen by and will recite his hamburger poem at the slightest provocation.

And it's working. People are coming to Seymour, not because it's a vacation spot, not because it's on the way to the Packer game, not even to golf. People are coming for the burgers, and Seymourians are proud of that, even prouder than Iowans are of Maid-Rites.

The Fletcher brothers were proud too. When they invented the Corny Dog in their Dallas garage in 1942, they sure as shootin' knew there was only one place for it to burst on the scene: the state fair of Texas. Fairgoers loved the handy combination of juicy hot dog sealed inside crisp cornbread casing, partly because it was tasty, and partly because it came from Texas. Competitive eating couple Rich and Carlene LeFevre ate thirty Corny Dogs between them to place first and second at the

184

fair the year I was a judge. They'd barely gulped their last wienie before gushing how delicious they were, and made right here in Dallas!

Certainly all three of these meaty meals are genuinely tasty. Their invention and popularization are logical and self-evident. And all three of these meats inspire immense pride in the places associated with them. But why?

In small towns especially, these meats exert a mystical power over their populations, turning everyone into traveling salespeople. Dissing Maid-Rites in Des Moines was like burning the flag. You can't get near the Fletcher Brothers Corny Dog booth without a cowboy hat on, and just try and get down the block in Seymour with Hamburger Charlie. Do people in small towns . . . feel small unless they're touting their meat?

Well, if they're relying on their meat for validation, we're in big trouble. Des Moines, Seymour, and Dallas are lucky their favorites are at least tasty. But there are other cities in America that for one reason or another have been forced to celebrate the rancid, the barely edible, the truly yucky. And I've been to all of them.

The meats of which I speak have no business on menus or in stomachs. Some are so obscure, marginal, or disgusting that all I could think about while chewing was, "Who was the first guy to conceive of eating this, and where is he buried?"

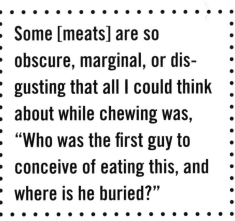

Some [meats] are so obscure, marginal, or disgusting that all I could think about while chewing was, "Who was the first guy to conceive of eating this, and where is he buried?"

Meats so ridiculously non-foodish, so far from the realm of "Hmmm, that looks tasty, maybe I'll pop that in my mouth and see if I enjoy its flavor," that only a Hell Week pledge could be excused for eating them on purpose.

But it was no fraternity rush on the range that spawned Rocky Mountain oysters. In truth, no one knows for sure why or when humans started eating cattle testicles, but we do know enough to blame the cowboys. So, in the absence of verifiable historical fact, I'm going to assume that this awful offal started as a macho cowboy dare.

Regardless of how the craze got started, there are still enough folks out there who enjoy them to keep them dangling on menus all across the West. I earned my "fuzzy dice" at The Fort in Morrison, Colorado, just outside Denver.

The Fort is like stepping back into the Wild West. Sam Arnold, the impresario of The Fort, built the place as a sort of replica of Bent's Fort, a fur trading outpost along the Santa Fe Trail circa 1840. Sam insisted on using the same kinds of adobe bricks used to build the original fort, and created an authentic location with a fantastic view to give modern people a chance to experience the Old West. Before his death, just months after our visit, Sam served traditional frontier foods from the period, including: salmon, beef, guinea pig, elk, and deliciously lean and tasty buffalo. Just like back in the day, no part of the bison goes unused: hump, tongue, sausage, not even the Rocky Mountain oysters are wasted.

Sam greeted me with a loud "Waugh!"—he said it scared away the grizzlies. It worked because there were none to be found in the dining room, just couples and families enjoying a vista that spanned the twinkling lights of Denver all the way

Rocky Mountain Oysters

Rocky Mountain Oysters: [n, plural]. Sometimes called Prairie Oysters, Toasted Yam Bag, Bull Beans, Cowboy Cojones, a North American culinary name for edible offal, specifically buffalo or bull testicles. Origin unknown.

to Pike's Peak. Sam asked me if I was thirsty, but before I could reply, he whipped out a bottle of champagne and tomahawked it open—with a real tomahawk. I don't usually drink at work, but Sam was just wild-eyed strange enough to convince me. It wasn't great champagne, but it was a sharp tomahawk.

We'd come to try Sam's reportedly delicious Rocky Mountain oysters. But I told him right from the get-go that I wasn't going to eat them. Sam harrumphed me, then cracked open a beef rib with a bowie knife—he was a rolling armory. He used the bowie to dig incredibly rich marrow butter out of the center of the bone, and spread it on some bread for me—it tasted like congealed grease from the bottom of a roast pan. Tasty, but one bite was enough for me. That pissed Sam off.

"Nonsense! It's delicious. All our food's natural and healthy for you!" screamed the wheelchair-bound, oxygen-tanked zealot. "I've been eating it all my life."

You had to love Sam. The twinkle in his eye—and the serrated knife in his hand—guaranteed that. He promised me the best steak I would ever have . . . after I finished my appetizer. The plate hit the table with a thud. They looked like deep-fried popcorn shrimp, but I knew they were really the golden brown sex organs of innocent bulls.

"Screw the Colonel, we got twice as many herbs and spices in our mix," Sam announced as he speared a chunk with the tip of his knife. "And you can taste every last one of 'em." He savored every bite, then offered me a chunk. I didn't want to hurt Sam's feelings, but I didn't want to eat his hairy buckeyes, either. I stalled.

"Sam, looks like you serve a lot of these. Where do you get them anyway?"

"Cowboys," he explained. "They cut 'em off the bulls to calm 'em down."

"Hmmm, you'd think it would have the exact opposite effect," I retorted to the delight of the waitstaff. But the moment Sam saw them smile he drove the knife deep into the table and pushed the plate of deep-fried giggle berries against my chest. The waiters stopped smiling, but I was still stalling.

"And what kind of cowboy does that? What's on his resume? How do you interview for a job like that?" I asked. "Who puts in forty hours a week yanking the nuggets off buffalos? Are the bulls sedated? Is the guy sedated? And where's his conscience? That has GOT to be a breach of Guy Code . . . "

I continued, but Sam was done. He rolled his chair away from the table and stared me down like I was a puma. He was our host on a packed Sunday, had cooked all kinds of delicious food, and damn it, I was gonna eat his saddle bags, or there was gonna be trouble.

Just then, the steak Sam had promised me arrived. From the smell alone, I knew he was right. The buffalo ribeye sizzled on the platter, beckoning to me from the far side of the oysters.

Sam moved the platter of lean yet marbled bison back and forth beneath my nose, but wouldn't let me touch it. Our eyes met, and I knew my shot clock was down to zero.

I grabbed a chunk and tossed it in my mouth. I chewed it once, then swallowed. Truthfully, it tasted like extra crispy KFC. I could barely taste the meat inside the crispy crust, and wasn't really keen on chewing enough to find out. I smiled at Sam.

"Open your mouth," he growled. I did, to prove it was all gone. "Well?"

"Well . . . they don't taste like what I thought bison testicle would taste like. And I don't have an uncontrollable urge to sing showtunes, so I guess I'm fine. Can I have my ribeye now?"

Sam growled back at me and slid the ribeye across the table. I took one bite and closed my eyes. It was the best steak I'd ever had. It was juicy, tender, succulent, flavorful . . . just typing these words is making my mouth salivate all over again. I've eaten in fine steakhouses all around the country, and Sam's buffalo rib-eye was the most flavorful, delicious meal I'd ever had.

To be completely truthful, the idea of the oysters turned out to be far worse than actually eating the morsels themselves. The idea that somewhere, some businessman was working on a spreadsheet designed to find ways to more efficiently harvest and market testicles as human food retched me out, but that ribeye made it all better.

Historically, many cultures around our world and in North America have made a habit of using all the parts of a butchered animal. By not wasting useful, if not delicious, protein like intestine and forehead meat, Chief Seattle believed we honor the life the animal chose to surrender to us by eating every last morsel of it. Waste was disrespectful to the spirit.

My travels have taught me that meat is a dialect. As I roam the country, each place sounds just a little different. The twang of Macon, Georgia, is not the same as the drawl in Austin, Texas. Our foods differ in much the same way. Depending on nothing more than where you're eating it, your hoagie is called a sub, grinder, hero, Italian, po'boy, wedge, zep, or torpedo.

I've also learned that meat has mystical powers:

- If bacon curls in a pan, a new lover is about to arrive.
- Finding a chicken egg with no yolk is unlucky.
- If meat shrinks in a pot, your downfall is assured. If it swells, you'll experience prosperity.
- Feed red pistachio nuts to a zombie—it will break his trance and allow him to die.

I know that last one wasn't about meat, but you should know it anyway, just in case. . . .

Earth's history is the story of meat. Chicken, fish, hoofed . . . we don't discriminate. If you can throw it on a Weber, we'll eat it. We cook and 'cue and blacken to achieve diversity in taste and nutrition, but it's all the same under the grill marks. Meat makes us human, literally.

> We cook and 'cue and blacken to achieve diversity in taste and nutrition, but it's all the same under the grill marks. Meat makes us human, literally.

Maybe that's why we eat the icky bits. Maybe deep in our DNA we know that any meat is better than no meat. Perhaps our bodies instinctively inspired the creativity that cooked up these carnivorous oddities to retain our precarious perch atop the food

chain. Maybe that's what the Maid-Rite groupies, the Fletcher brothers, and Hamburger Bill are so proud of: After millions of years of surviving with the fittest, we're still here.

WWW.HOMEOFTHEHAMBURGER.ORG

SEYMOUR'S OWN
Original Charlie Burger Recipe
  1 pound ground beef (80–85 percent lean)
  ⅓ cup bread crumbs
  1 large egg, slightly beaten
  ¼ cup diced union
  1 teaspoon pepper
  1 teaspoon salt

½ stick of butter (⅛ pound)
1 pickle spear

1. Combine ground beef, bread crumbs, egg, onion, pepper, and salt in a mixing bowl and mix thoroughly. Form into three patties using your hands for molding.
2. Preheat fry pan or griddle and melt the butter in the pan. Place burgers in pan and cook over medium heat. Brown until liquid starts to turn brownish.
3. Turn burgers and cook until well done (160°F). Insert a thermometer to determine the temperature.
4. Remove from pan and place on a lightly buttered, lightly toasted, thick-sliced bread. (A Kaiser roll or bun can also be used.)
5. Add pickle for garnish. Serve with your favorite chips or fries and beverage.

Note: Never press down on a burger while it is cooking as that will squeeze the juices out.

Charlie's Chant:

Hamburger, hamburger, hamburger hot,
with an onion in the middle and a pickle on top,
makes your lips go flippity flop.
Come on over, try an order.
Fried in butter, listen to it sputter.

MAD DOG AND MERRILL: HAMBURGER KABOBS

You will need:

- 7 quarter-pound hamburgers
- 7 slices of your favorite cheese
- 7 hamburger buns

Various toppings for each hamburger (pickles, onions, olives, sauerkraut, peppers, pickle relish, barbecue sauce, lettuce, bacon, mushrooms—whatever toppings you like)

1. Grill hamburgers to your desired doneness.
2. Top each burger with your favorite cheese. Close grill cover for 2–3 minutes so cheese can melt.
3. Take burgers off the grill and place them on bun and top each burger with your favorite toppings.
4. (You will need 4 metal skewers at least 16" long and an additional 4 sets of hands to assist.) Stack burgers on top of each other. Place the 4 skewers through the stack of hamburgers so you will be able to cut the burgers in fourths.
5. Slice the stack of burgers in fourths and serve.

Serves 4 hungry people.

Enjoy.

COURTESY OF GARY MERRILL

Chapter 12
Tell 'Em I Sent Ya

If you're doing it right, having fun is exhausting. But living on the road can also be lonely and repetitive. By necessity, we were constantly inventing provocative amusements to have some laughs. The next time you find yourself stuck on a boring business trip, try some of my favorites:

HOTEL LOBBY WIFFLE BALL—We'd recruit strangers and play baseball around the furniture. Game time was midnight because at that hour, it was easier to convince strangers to play. It's also prime pizza delivery time. Ask the desk clerk who makes the best pizza around and order a few. When the delivery guy arrives, challenge him to a game, double or nothing. He wins, you pay twice, he loses, all he gets is a tip. It's a great way to try some local pie, and exercise at the same time.

THE ELEVATOR SHOW—I sat on Big Blue, my luggage, in an elevator and hosted a talk show as people got on and off. My goal was to get them to ride as many up/down cycles as possible, talking about their trip, their job, whatever was on their minds. One night we had a security guard, a couple from Auckland, two kids at prom, and a pro bowler in the Four Seasons elevator for six cycles. Good show.

BUSINESS CARD—Everyone I meet slips me their business card. Instead of tossing them, I keep them in Big Blue.

Then when we're out playing Brian, we take turns pulling cards at random. You have to convince at least one stranger you are whoever you pulled, complete with an improvised job description, family, and reason why you're on this trip. If you fool at least one local, you drink free all night. If you fail, you buy all night. It's a great way to instigate conversation with strangers, and also a hilarious way to practice the fine art of bullshit. My personal triumphs include convincing a nun I was Jack Hoffner, a bourbon distiller who'd won a regional Jazzercise championship and was in town for Nationals. I was also Carl Schumburg, a PR director for Spam, giving a keynote address at a Vegan Franchisees symposium; Gary "Lefty" Gordon, a kleptomaniac catfish farmer; and Trace Courtnall, an FDA biologist who was afraid of open spaces. After we are sure the victim has been fooled, we let them in on the joke and let them pull the next card. There is NO better way to kill a night than getting an entire hotel bar to pretend they're somebody else, one stranger at a time.

Travel is about POV. So no matter where we landed, I made it my job to mingle. Talking to strangers, seeing shows, and eating new foods was my life. Packing, checking in, and watching the seatbelt demo with a straight face was my job. And the fun didn't stop when we turned off the cameras. Our new friends would often whisk us through their city after work, staging a personalized gauntlet of hilarity that made the whole day feel like its own separate show. Those were the nights I remember, the stories in this book: the adventures that transformed me into a Road Warrior.

It's an elite fraternity. Yes, there's a life back home, family, friends, and things to do. But the minute the cabin door closes, all of it goes into suspended animation, leaving only The Road. By necessity, I found myself embracing all the transitory spaces and people that filled my days. Hotel lobbies were living rooms, airports were offices, restaurants were kitchens. The alternative would have been to live in virtual isolation for months at a time, and would have pissed away the most entertaining and humbling time of my life. I was stunned to admit that after more than three decades of life, I had much to learn . . . especially about doughnuts.

If you weren't looking for Voodoo Doughnuts, you'd never find it. The shop sits in Old Town, "the crotch of Portland (Oregon)," on a street filled with bars and trendy clubs, not a Starbucks in sight. A small wooden door is the only wormhole between the real world and the arch universe of Tres and Cat Daddy.

Tres Shannon and Kenneth "Cat Daddy" Pogson had been friends a long time before deciding to

COURTESY OF VOODOO DOUGHNUT, TRAVEL PORTLAND

open their doughnut shop. They'd never run a shop and didn't know how to make doughnuts, but they didn't let that stop them from taking a pilgrimage to Southern California to learn. Upon their return to Oregon, they took Portland by storm, and began creating treats perfectly suited for the altered states of consciousness of most of their late night patrons.

Dirty Snowballs and the Old Dirty Bastard are just two of their big sellers, but my personal favorite was the Memphis Mafia—a fritter the size of your head, covered with chocolate chips, banana, and peanut butter. Eating one of these makes you feel just like Elvis . . . five minutes before he died.

Families eat doughnuts for breakfast; the "in crowd" eats them as a nightcap. So that we'd capture the essence of the late night Voodoo experience, a pair of local hipsters agreed to stage their very own Voodoo Wedding for our cameras. Cat Daddy, who just happens to be a registered minister, would perform the ceremony, while Tres handled the doughnuts and the guests, making sure not to smear the latter with the former.

> **My personal favorite was the Memphis Mafia—a fritter the size of your head, covered with chocolate chips, banana, and peanut butter. Eating one of these makes you feel just like Elvis . . . five minutes before he died.**

Unlike the Elvis Chapel Wedding we visited in Vegas, the Voodoo Wedding somehow was able to embrace, yet not be tarred by, its cheesy kitsch. Both were equally contrived events,

COURTESY OF VOODOO DOUGHNUT, TRAVEL PORTLAND

both reveled in their audacity, but only the Voodoo "I do's" rang true. After spending a few hours with Tres and Cat Daddy, I realized that unlike their trendy Melrose Avenue doppelgangers in California, these guys weren't pretending to be weird because it's cool. They were just weird. And instead of running away to join the circus, they built their own, complete with a clown car full of guests.

As midnight struck, Portland's unapologetically strange arrived in pairs, dressed in outlandish outfits as if they were boarding Andy Warhol's ark. The vibe was more art opening than church wedding, but it worked. It was the most romantic doughnut shop I'd ever been in. The betrothed were crazy in love and were thrilled to be tying the knot in the refracted light of the slowly turning display case. Tonight's couple had picked the "Deluxe Legal Voodoo Wedding," even though Cat offered a wide variety of other ceremonies, ranging from the $25 "Intentional Commitment" ceremony (doughnuts and coffee for six, no parking) up through the $4,500 "Whole Shebang." Doughy vows were exchanged along with kisses, and then it was time for the Wedding Doughnuts—eclairs served inside the doughnuts much the same way trains enter a tunnel.

After the wedding, the happy couple went on their honeymoon, while we stayed behind to make the doughnuts. Tres walked me through every step with the same enthusiasm and commitment he brings to every day behind his counter. I felt like I was interning at the Cirque du Soleil breakfast nook. And even in the middle of the night, the process was an eye opener.

> As midnight struck, Portland's unapologetically strange arrived in pairs, dressed in outlandish outfits as if they were boarding Andy Warhol's ark. The vibe was more art opening than church wedding, but it worked. It was the most romantic doughnut shop I'd ever been in.

Unlike lutefisk, doughnuts are harder to make than they are to eat. First, we mixed up the Voodoo "secret" batter, then rolled out all the shapes and sizes we'd need to create their masterpieces. The shapes took some time to rise, kind of like bread, before we dropped them into the hot oil where they'd float until Tres pronounced them "done."

That's when the real fun began. Salty and sweet work together, sticky and smooth too. Maple, ginger, fruit—tubs of treats were everywhere, like being in Willy Wonka's garage. We stuffed the "blanks" with maple syrup, peanut butter, crème, cream, crème fraîche, and whatever else was in grabbing distance.

Aside from the doughnuts you'd expect, Tres and Cat Daddy have a knack for marrying flavors that don't sound like they should even go out as "just friends." Tubs of every conceivable edible lined the wall, Cap'n Crunch (with and without Crunch Berries) were located adjacent to bananas and bacon, in a filing system understood only by the staff.

Grape Ape is a raised doughnut with vanilla frosting and grape powder . . . there's a grape powder? The Neapolitan features a chocolate doughnut with vanilla frosting and strawberry Quik powder. And in a purposefully ironic twist, the Powdered Sugar doughnut . . . isn't available. No request is too strange, no ingredient too bizarre for the doughnut dudes. We tried virtually everything in their shining, swirling Plexiglas doughnut tower, and nothing was less than outstanding.

Tres and Cat Daddy win. Many people never get to that lofty place, stuck working jobs they hate, enduring lives instead of living them. I don't know that I'd fly to Portland just for a doughnut, but I do know that when I return, I'll head back to Voodoo for a redo on my mojo. If you beat me there, tell 'em I sent ya.

A week later we were in Battle Creek, Michigan, dancing with Tigers and watching ducks wrestle. The event was the 50th Annual Battle Creek CerealFest, and all our heroes were there. I danced with Tony the Tiger, talked politics with Fred Flintstone, and got the reigning Cereal Queen to do a cartwheel inside the Kellogg's factory. But life in the cereal capital of the world wasn't always so sweet.

It all began in 1895 when inventor C.W. Post brought the first breakfast cereal to market. "Postum" was a cereal beverage, a drinkable suspension of grain and liquid that established an entirely new industry, and a new benchmark for "yucky."

Two years later, he struck gold by marketing one of the first ready-to-eat breakfast cereals—in the form we all know and slurp today—Grape Nuts. Named for the "grape sugar" that

formed during the baking of the grain and their nutty taste, the cereal was easy to transport, easy to store, and easy to prepare. A far cry from traditional breakfasts of the day that required loading fresh wood into the stove, a round-trip to the henhouse, and an aerobic workout to slice fatback off the pork slab, Grape Nuts were easy and cheap, and were promoted as a "health food," alongside Battle Creek resorts famous for magical rejuvenating properties. It's been over a hundred years, but Battle Creek is still the epicurean epicenter of morning num-nums.

To prove it, we ate breakfast downtown on the World's Longest Breakfast Table, helping volunteers serve five tons of cereal, two semi-trucks of milk, seventy thousand bananas, and eighty thousand voodoo-free doughnut holes. Detroit has their auto show, L.A. has its Consciousness Expo, and every year Battle Creek lays out America's biggest breakfast. It was an honor to officiate the event, even though there were a few heated discussions over the correct milk/cereal ratio. After burying that spoon, we shot the factory tour, flipped the beauty queen, and only needed one more shot to hit the road and make our plane.

Each year CerealFest raises money for charity with its Ken-Ducky Derby. Contributors buy one of a thousand yellow rubber duckies that get loaded into a giant cereal box suspended by a crane over Battle Creek. To start the Derby, the Main Duck (a guy in a duck suit) pulls a long rope attached to the giant cereal box, dumping the duckies into the creek. He then quacks appropriately as the duckies float downstream toward the finish line. The first duckie to cross it wins a prize for its owner.

Tipping the duckies into the creek is a simple task, if you have a rudimentary knowledge of mechanics. Unfortunately, the Main Duck did not. He appeared at the appointed hour, row-

My Favorite . . . CIVIC FESTIVAL
Taste of Chicago
Chicago's Lakefront at Grant Park
Ten Days, Ending on the Fourth of July

Civic Festival? Yes, I'm calling this something different because I couldn't pick a favorite between Jazz Fest and Taste. Don't hate, I do it for you.

In my travels, I've developed an excellent sense of mojo. When a city is particularly vibrant or alive, I can actually sense its energy walking off the plane. Seriously. You could blindfold me, and before I got into the terminal, there are probably twenty cities I can ID just by feel. Most prominent on that list is Chicago.

I was born there, perhaps that has something to do with it. But the city also has an undeniable vibe that permeates every inch of its perfectly laid out, impossible to get lost in, grid.

Chicagoans have a no-nonsense approach to life that sets us apart from New Yorkers, southerners, even the Amish. We spend eight months a year cowering under three feet of snow or sweltering in 100 percent humidity. So when it's nice outside, Chicagoans party down.

Taste of Chicago, staged at the always "cooler near the lake" Grant Park, marks the middle of summer with headline music, and booths filled with sample sizes of the city's best tastes. Go early, buy your food tickets—admission is free—and gorge. Then when you're too stuffed to move, throw your blanket on the Petrillo lawn and groove to the music. My ears are never happier than those summer nights that mix the sounds from acts like Stevie Wonder with shouts from guys named Stosh from Berwyn.

If you're coming in from out of town, get a hotel south of the Chicago River and near Grant Park to avoid the year's worst traffic. Before you walk back to your room at night, sit under a tree, close your eyes, and feel Chicago. Gets your mojo workin'.

ing into view in his canoe. He dropped anchor under the bridge where the giant cereal box hung. But then things went awry.

The Main Duck grabbed the rope attached to the top of the giant cereal box, and yanked to release the duckies and start the Derby.

But the giant box wouldn't tip. Main Duck yanked harder, rocking his canoe violently. I'm no Einstein, but it looked like the rope had been fastened too high up the side of the box and now that it was filled, it was too heavy for just one duck to empty it. Sadly, the entire debacle played out fifteen feet from the banks of the creek where hundreds of fresh-faced youngsters waited for their ducks to begin the race.

After another titanic tug, Main Duck did the unthinkable; he leapt out of his canoe into the raging river . . . revealing it was really only a foot deep. Our crew, three local news crews, and a growing gaggle of gawkers chewed our collective lips to keep from laughing at this poor guy, knee deep in a muddy duck costume, yanking on a rope like the Hunchback of Battle Creek.

A final mighty tug flipped the canoe and landed Main Duck on his tail in the shallow water. The explosion of laughter echoed

Our crew, three local news crews, and a growing gaggle of gawkers chewed our collective lips to keep from laughing at this poor guy, knee deep in a muddy duck costume, yanking on a rope like the Hunchback of Battle Creek.

off the cement-lined waterway like a cannon blast. Main Duck did not share our glee. He turned to the crowd and gave us a look. How he did this from inside the suit, I'm not sure, but he forced a hush over the crowd . . . until, from the grassy knoll, the agonized voice of a ten-year-old boy rang out:

"Pull the rope, you pussy!"

The Main Duck spun toward the kid and made a gesture. The kid screamed back. Parents ridiculed the Duck. The taunting mounted, but before the Duck climbed ashore to beak someone, the crane driver twisted the rope and the giant cereal box released its flotilla.

A cheer erupted on Battle Creek. Without missing a beat, the Main Duck shook off the mud like a Labrador, took a bow, and rowed away.

Over the past few years as Michigan's fortunes have declined, attendance at CerealFest has eroded dramatically. The event used to set a new world record every year for Biggest Breakfast, but now empty storefronts line Main Street and people show up more for food than folly. Main Duck knew this fifty-year tradition was in tatters. It would have been easy for him to just throw in the towel and quack off. But Main Duck chose instead to be a hero. Faced with an impossible task, irascible fans, and with the fate of an inspirational charity literally hanging in the balance, the nameless winged avenger never gave up, making sure to deliver the goods before heading south for lunch. If you're ever in Michigan the second weekend of June, scoot over to Battle Creek for an all too balanced breakfast. And if you happen to run into the Main Duck, tell 'em I sent ya.

If you're like me, you love live music. 'Course, if you are like me, you knew that already. Far and away, the best place to find random musical genius is on Bourbon Street in New Orleans. Chicago's North Side is stacked with genuine joints, as are Austin, Nashville, San Francisco, and Boston. I've heard literally hundreds of working bands all across the country, but there is one that stands above them all. But unless you live in Memphis, you've never heard of them.

Yes, Memphis. Birthplace of rock 'n' roll, home of Sun Studios where Elvis, Jerry Lee, Johnny Cash, and Carl Perkins got their start. Memphis is America's other musical Mississippi River town and Beale Street is its soul.

Beale always beat the pulse of the city, even before 1947 when Riley King hitchhiked north from Itta Bena, Mississippi, to tour the world as B. B. King.

But Beale is no Branson nostalgia stop, filled with bluehairs and early dinner specials. It's a vibrant chunk of funk with the best food and music in Tennessee, including the fried peanut butter and banana sandwiches available down the road at Graceland.

Ribs feed Memphis; the town is evenly split between apostles of the Rendezvous famous dry rub ribs, and the stellar wet ribs sold by the truckload around the corner at the Blues City Café. Both types of spareribs, along with every other kind of southern food, simmer up and down Beale all year long. During the summer, Wednesday is biker night when the street is closed to traffic and leather-clad bad-asses from all over the South show up to devour barbecue and boogie to the best sound in town. All of it, the food and the tunes, are packed into just three blocks of genuine joints like: the Rum Boogie Café, Beale Street Tap Room, the Black Diamond, King's Palace Café, the New Daisy Theatre, the Pig on Beale, The Shake Shack, B. B. King's Blues Club, and Dyer's Burgers, where they proudly advertise that they haven't changed the fry grease since 1912. Oh, they've added to it, they've transported it, but it's never been completely emptied and refilled. Try the fries and eat like Ben Hooper, Tennessee's turn-of-the-century bastard governor.

Regardless of the sides, it's ribs that soothe the savage beast. Memphis is a two-shift town. Beale's meat masters are just starting their day when the musicians pack it up around 3:00 or 4:00 a.m. It takes a long time to make raw pork into succulent meat so tender it literally drops off the bone when you make a point. But that's what makes Memphis ribs famous.

The Rendezvous was born in 1948 when Charlie Vergos cleaned out the basement beneath his deli and found a coal chute. They've been using the same brick oven ever since. It starts early every morning when the wood and mesquite is loaded into the oven to get the heat just right for the meat that's been aging in nearby coolers. The barbecue master applies the Rendezvous special mix of dry herbs and seasoning, massaging it into the meat like a Swedish spa attendant. They work for hours on meat that lasts but a few minutes after it's dropped on the table. Unlike most ribs, the Rendezvous Ribs are not served swimming in red sauce, but rather dry with dipping options. Patrons say they want to taste the meat, not the sauce. Besides, if you like a "wet rib," you do have options.

The Blues City Café is the other famous rib joint in Memphis. Located on the corner of Beale and 2nd, across from the B. B. King Blues Club, where patrons are encouraged to "Put some South in your Mouth" on a nightly basis. Blues City ribs are wet ribs, soaked in a tangy, zippy sauce and served in a loud and colorful diner. In Chicago the enduring battle is Cubs/Sox; in Memphis it's Rendezvous/Blues City. Ideally, you stay in Memphis long enough to try both.

But if you have to choose only one, Blues City does have one advantage: dinner and a show. Anchoring America's Boulevard of Boogie, you're just steps away from the greatest bar band in the land when you push your bloated belly away from the table and waddle one storefront east.

All of the local clubs have great house bands that jump, jive, and thrive pumping out Beale's boogie, but only one rules the rue. It's the band that fills the Blues City Café every night and doesn't leave until the audience is panting and spent. A band you've never heard of . . . until now.

The Dempseys are the best bar band I've ever seen. A rockabilly trio featuring upright bass, snare, and ridiculous guitar work, they burn down the house every night. Each of their sets concludes with a dance floor filled with panting, sweaty people. The same people that only an hour before were unbuckling their belts to accommodate their ribs are somehow motivated to get up and boogie down. Think about that. You've been "rib-full" before. You know that all you want to do is lie down and moan

> You've been "rib-full" before. You know that all you want to do is lie down and moan with pleasure, yet night after night, these musical chameleons are able to invigorate a listless crowd and make the dance floor buckle.

with pleasure, yet night after night, these musical chameleons are able to invigorate a listless crowd and make the dance floor buckle.

One of the many things that make the Dempseys great is that everyone plays everything. Halfway through their set, the drummer moves to bass, the bass player moves to guitar, and the guitarist gets behind the drums . . . without missing a beat, literally. Then, twenty minutes later, they do it again, this time while the bass player stands on top of his bass. (You can get their music and schedule at www.thedempseys.net). The Dempseys don't tour; you must go to the Dempseys. They play everything you want to hear, and do it like their hair is on fire. But don't just take my word for it. Listen to the late Sam Phillips, founder of Sun Records and producer for Elvis Presley, Jerry Lee Lewis, Johnny Cash, Roy Orbison, Carl Perkins, and many others. "I swear to God, The Dempseys are the greatest I've ever heard!"

The next time you are within one hundred miles of Memphis, get to Beale Street. And if you have a chance to talk to The Dempseys before they vibrate off into another dimension, tell 'em I sent ya.

The history of our country is written in hot sauce. Back in the day, each region of the country only served the meats and vegetables that were geographically available . . . and easily caught. Advances in transportation and refrigeration not only birthed the Key lime and Eskimo Pies, but also mixed up our American gumbo. Yet over a century later, there are still a few culinary cul-de-sacs and unspoiled menus that retain their original flavors. Like soul food.

It don't get more South than Athens, Georgia. Launching pad of R.E.M. and the B-52s, Athens is Atlanta's hip little brother. Like Iowa City and Austin, this college town is a magnet for all the "alternative" kids escaping from family farms to try and find their own soul. Luckily, there is a gastro-pastor to lead them to the promised land.

Proprietor and self-proclaimed Professor of Soul, Dexter Weaver calls his restaurant Weaver D's Delicious Fine Foods, "Because I am, and it is." "It" is also a small, white shack within walking distance of campus, bursting with hungry seekers every day from dawn to dusk. By six, Weaver and his two helpers have turned out so much soul food they just gotta stop and charge their funk up.

COURTESY OF PAMELA SCHNEIDER

Weaver D is part preacher, part chef, and all energy. His motto hangs over the door and was immortalized in 1994 on

R.E.M.'s Grammy-nominated album, *Automatic for the People*. But just what does that mean, exactly?

"It's automatic," beams Weaver during the brief lull between his late breakfast and early lunch crush. "When people come here we will always provide fine foods at an optimally set price that is pleasing to both the customer and us. Customer service is the only thing. 'Automatic for the People' means we'll always be ready, quick, and efficient."

Weaver's recipes of traditional southern soul food are both original and timeless, and his side dishes of mantra and aphorism keep the line of hungry but polite customers humming happily through his joint. We showed up to taste his highly touted squash casserole. Why, I couldn't tell you.

Do you know anyone who actually likes squash? Anyone under seventy who'd choose squash over peas or carrots or spinach even? Especially in a college town. That's one of the main reasons I WENT to college, to never again eat brussels sprouts or cabbage rolls. You'd think the students would be standing in line for ox tail, ribs, and some of Weaver's tasty sandwiches. Wouldn't you?

COURTESY OF PAMELA SCHNEIDER

Weaver D knew we were coming and promised to cook the best squash casserole of his life. His James Beard cooking award hung around his neck like an Olympic medal and his kitchen was spotless, no small trick for an ancient place out in the woods. He was proud of his awards, proud of his famous rock star customers, but mostly, proud of his food. He couldn't stop talking about all the fresh ingredients he used, and how his recipes kept everyone coming back again and again.

I asked him what made his squash "soul food." He laughed in my face.

"'Course you don't know what soul food is," he chided me. "That means you don't got no soul. No soul at all. That's why you're here, to get some soul from me!"

"Just because I'm white, I don't got soul?"

"No. Just because you don't got no soul means you don't got soul. But it's okay, that's why He brought you here today. To get some."

Just so you know, dear reader, I'm one of the hippest guys I know. Humble too. I've been a musician for fifteen years, been in every blues club across the country, and can even cook cornbread. What the hell?

"You come here, asking me about soul food," the self-anointed preacher said, shaking his head. "If you knew, you'd have. Since you don't, you don't."

"You are crazy! Most of my iTunes library was recorded by people of color. Al Green, Nina Simone, James Brown, Solomon Burke, Wynonie Harris, Neville Brothers, Earth, Wind, and Fire, Sinatra (part Sicilian), Junior Wells, B. B., Buddy Guy, Muddy . . . "

I turned to find myself six inches from Weaver's face, and that's when it hit me. This southern preacher/poacher, this lyrical mojo-maker was a dead ringer for the Hoochie Coochie Man himself.

" . . . Waters."

Weaver wasn't impressed by my lyrical litany, didn't even react. He just kept cooking. Maybe he and Muddy were secretly related and I'd embarrassed him. It wasn't really a stretch. Mud was from Mississippi, only one state away from Georgia. The scenario is easy to imagine. Those early bluesmen did a lot of traveling, especially through their native South. Muddy in particular was very vocal about his admiration and attraction to young members of the feminine persuasion. Songs like "Nineteen," "Hello Little Girl," and "Gypsy Woman" blared his appetites to the world, much like Weaver D's lunch-counter rants filled his hall with rhythmic sound set to the clicky-clack of his meat cleaver.

So just because they didn't share the same last name was no reason to suspect I was wrong, I just had to be tactful. I was sure he'd heard it a million times, but when the cameras turned off, I took him aside to ask him one more time.

"First of all, I do too have soul," I said, my feelings still bruised. "Second, I think you know the Gypsy Woman." Not a flutter passed over his face. Nothing. He just kept talking about his squash.

"Everything in here gotta be double whipped," he said, oblivious to my line of questioning. "Just keep turning and twirling your wrist, like you're spinning a lariat."

He didn't even look down; he knew that it didn't feel ready. So he kept whipping. Oblivious or evasive, I couldn't tell, so I just blurted it out.

"Are you related to Muddy Waters?"

Then, Mr. Soul Food lost his title.

"Muddy who?"

"Muddy Waters? McKinley Morganfield?" I searched his eyes for even a glimmer of recognition. "Father of Chicago Blues. First recorded by Alan Lomax in Stovall, Mississippi, August 1941. The Rolling Stones named their band after him, the grandfather of rock and roll . . . THAT Muddy Waters."

"I never heard of him."

I was incredulous. Apoplectic. And all the other things anyone with a decent music collection would have been. After spending twenty minutes telling me all the reasons I didn't have soul, this dead-ringer for my favorite dead singer made a mockery out of his argument. Even worse, he didn't even know how wrong he was. How could the author of the cult-classic *Automatic, Y'All, Weaver D's Guide to the Soul* be so vacant on the most soulful singer the South had ever birthed? And worse, how could he turn around and accuse me of his crime? We kept cooking in silence, and for the first time in my travels, I was deeply, truly hurt.

I dropped the issue and just finished the segment. We ate Weaver's squash casserole, which he somehow made delicious. It was buttery, nutty, and went perfectly with the barbecue and mac 'n' cheese he laid out for our lunch. From a cacophony of crud, he'd orchestrated a fluffy masterpiece.

While I was ripping the meat off the bone, I secretly sent a production assistant to a local record store to get me a CD for dessert. I slipped it into the boom box and hit play.

The unmistakable opening riff of "Hoochie Coochie Man" thundered through the closed restaurant.

Dun Da do do DUM
Gypsy woman told my mother
Dun Da do do DUM
Got a Boy Child comin', gon' be a son of a gun.

Everyone in the place instantly recognized the song. Everyone but Weaver. It was my turn to minister now.

"THAT is Muddy Waters," I said, turning up the box.

Weaver sat and listened for a moment. A smile of recognition finally spread across that Muddy face of his. I pulled the CD case out of my pocket and handed it to him.

"Muddy invented soul."

Weaver listened to a few more famous bars, then turned to me with a smile.

"I was wrong. You do got it."

And that was it. We dug back into his grub and listened to the soundtrack of the day, at least the one that had been playing in my head. Halfway through "Mannish Boy," Weaver turned to me.

"I remind you of him? Lord! I gotta be doing something right. Automatic!"

If you're ever in Athens, Georgia, before 6:00 p.m. and have a hankering for a generous portion of soul to chew on, make your way down to 1016 E. Broad Street and get you some. And if that CD is playing when you walk in, sing along as loud as you can. And if it isn't, make sure you tell Weaver D I sent ya so he can fix that.

In the process of saving Dexter's soul, we learned that true soul food takes an appreciation of history, a knack in the kitchen, and a complete disregard for the Atkins diet. It also requires a thick gravy.

The Coffee Cup was a small, simple diner on the edge of Charlotte, North Carolina. The counter had been serving blacks and whites side by side longer than any other place in town, and just happens to boast an original southern staple. That's why we pulled up early one Friday morning to find Gardine Wilson, the Coffee Cup's newish owner, at the door. His eyes lit up as he explained The Cup opened in 1947, became integrated in 1968, and received National Historical Landmark designation in 2007. He was proud of his food and excited about his plans for the future. He also explained the secret of his success. It wasn't him, it wasn't the décor or unlimited vacant lot parking, it was the secret weapon stashed away in the kitchen. He informed me that I would be one of the few northerners lucky enough to gain admission to her queendom.

Though ownership of the landmark had changed many times over the past two decades, control of the stove had not. Gardine explained that without the lady behind the skillet, the joint would've been part of the vacant lot by now. She's a woman with a hearty laugh, a naughty sense of humor, and the best Red Eye Gravy in all of Charlotte. Just ask her.

"What you wanna see?" she drawled as I dared approach her stove.

"How about breakfast," I said.

Then she went to work. Miss Theresa's signature vein-clogging elixir is made by combining ham drippings, coffee, and flour, thus giving the gravy a dark red color that's perfect for biscuits, breakfasts, and boogie. She pulled me to the stove and started teaching.

"Pay attention and you'll learn something," she purred. "I seen your show. You never do any cookin', just stand around while everybody else does the work. Lemme tell you something, and listen good, ladies love a man who cooks. That's right."

Miss Theresa grabbed an ancient cast iron skillet and threw it on a burner turned up full. She took a Folgers can and poured some bacon and/or ham grease from that morning's breakfast into the skillet and swished it around as it began to sizzle. Then she added coffee and flour, stirred it a bit, then just watched as little bubbles started to pop all through the thickening mixture.

"This is gonna change your life," she assured me.

I didn't have the heart to say her doughy grease wasn't going to make me speak in tongues. Instead, I was polite and waited for her mixture to brown. It took awhile.

"What's the best breakfast you ever ate?" she asked.

"Who knows," I said, "It's just breakfast."

"Then get ready," she smirked. "'Cause this is it."

"I seriously doubt biscuits and gravy is gonna take the Gold," I said, cranky 'cause she wasted the coffee in the gravy instead of in me. "I mean, it smells great, and looks different, but I've had some good breakfasts in my day."

"Name three."

I couldn't.

Chuckling to herself, Miss Theresa took some biscuits, poured her savory sauce all over them, then plopped the dish down in front of me, grinning like a six-year-old at the circus. She knew exactly what was coming next. But I had no idea.

I really try and avoid greasy, fatty foods. If I ate all the fried foods I've been offered in our travels, I'd look like a novelty arena zeppelin. You know, the blimp that flies around between periods at a hockey game just inches over the heads of the fans, dropping candy and gift cards. One of those . . . without the pro-

pellers, but with shoes. That's what I'd be, and clearly it would be problematic. That's why I usually just take my courtesy bite, then slyly put down the plate and move away.

One bite of Miss Theresa's gravy was not enough. I ate both biscuits . . . and asked for seconds.

I cannot describe the velvety deliciousness or how perfectly the blend of fresh biscuits and creamy gravy melted on my tongue like bacon-flavored candy. I knew enough of these could kill me, but really, what's the harm in one morning of decadence? I'd do an extra set of hotel lunges later. I literally licked the plate. Miss Theresa caught me, threw her head back, and laughed.

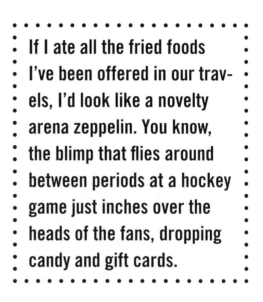

If I ate all the fried foods I've been offered in our travels, I'd look like a novelty arena zeppelin. You know, the blimp that flies around between periods at a hockey game just inches over the heads of the fans, dropping candy and gift cards.

"I told you. And I knew you didn't believe me . . . they never do. But I'm right, right?"

She's more than right. Miss Theresa is a voodoo alchemist, turning grease into gold every morning before the sun comes up. Her breakfast was so good, funky soul music started throbbing out of the radio, bouncing against the cinder block walls of the kitchen. Without missing a beat, Miss Theresa turned to me.

"Can you at least dance?"

I grabbed her hips and spun her away from the stove. Rather than squirm away—the usual reaction when I try to dance with a woman—she ground her hips into mine and we shook it. Al Green was singing, gravy was sizzling, and Miss Theresa was working me like a rented mule. It turned into a game of Chicken: neither one of us was gonna stop grinding before the other, so we just kept dancing. By the time the song ended, we were sweaty and I was hungry again.

"Not bad," she grinned as she made me another plate of hammy ambrosia. I devoured the food before the plate stopped rattling and gave her a big hug.

There is a genuine sweetness about Miss Theresa that is intoxicating. Like a lot of people who choose to go into the food service business, she has an honest love of feeding people, and providing them with comfort of every kind. If you "are what you eat" there are a lot of Charlotte-ans walking around with big chunks of Miss Theresa in 'em. She's a fixture in the city, much like The Cup itself, responsible for lifetimes of happy meals and sweet memories.

I called Miss Theresa to tell her about this book, but learned her phone had been disconnected. In the wake of the 2008 recession, the original Coffee Cup closed its doors in November, never to reopen. The economy ravaged their business, and eventually Gardine just couldn't survive. All that's left now is the vacant lot. And even though I knew her for just one dance, I feel like my Cup is gone too. But I promise you, the next time someone asks me about the best breakfast I ever had, I'll have an answer.

Thankfully, Miss Theresa wasn't out of work for long. After being closed for months, Gardine was finally able to secure a new location and throw open his doors in mid-2009. The new Coffee Cup is about a mile east of town, but still has the same

old magic. So if you are ever east of the city and happen to run into the one queen of the cup, make sure you tell her I sent ya.

O.D.B. RECIPE
Old Dirty Bastard
Take a raised yeast doughnut and dip in chocolate. Put Oreos on top and drizzle with peanut butter.

MEMPHIS MAFIA RECIPE

1. Take whatever leftover dough you have from your other doughnuts. Mix in chocolate, bananas, and peanut butter and chop up.
2. Ball up, flatten, and place on a frying screen. Fry each side until done.
3. Let fritters cool and glaze. Drizzle hot peanut butter and chocolate on the top of each and throw on some peanuts and chocolate chips!

SQUASH CASSEROLE
WEAVER D'S, ATHENS, GEORGIA
5 pounds yellow squash

1 medium onion, diced

1 stick Parkay margarine

1 teaspoon salt

1 teaspoon garlic salt

½ of a 10¾-ounce can of Campbell's condensed mushroom soup

3 large eggs

1½ cup sharp cheese

1 teaspoon black pepper

1. Preheat oven to 350°F.

2. Slice and boil squash in a pan of water, then put in colander to drain.
3. Sauté onion in 1 stick of Parkay.
4. Put drained squash in bowl and add Parkay margarine and onion, salt, garlic salt, mushroom soup, eggs, sharp cheese, and pepper; stir all together.
5. Put in 3-quart casserole dish. Bake at 350°F for 1½ hours.

Serves 14.

COURTESY OF WEAVER D.

Chapter 13
TDW

The Three-Day Weekend (TDW) road trip is uniquely American, the modern equivalent of rolling with Lewis and Clark—only instead of virgin wilderness teeming with undiscovered flora, fauna, and strange people, we've got it all on Google Earth. This century, the undiscovered stuff is hard to come by, unless you're looking for strange people. No matter which direction you want to drive, there's plenty of weirdos within one tank of gas of wherever you are right now. Especially if you get snared, like I did, in the seven-state net of the rootin'est, tootin'est cash cow east of the Pecos.

I've enjoyed beef in all its forms: Chicago's Italian beef sangwiches, homemade jerky in Phoenix, Vegas's nine-pound hamburger, Hamburger Charlie's more modest portion slathered in butter, and the surprisingly

tasty pitchfork fondue in Montana. There's certainly no shortage of fine steak houses around the country, but sometimes they can be hard to find unless you know the right people. Then again, sometimes it's not so hard.

You don't find Amarillo's Big Texan Free 72 oz. Steak Ranch by accident, you are badgered into a pilgrimage by the billboards. If you've ever driven more than a hundred yards on I-40, or US 287, US 87, US 60, or I-27, you've succumbed. There's no such thing as a free lunch . . . unless you're in Texas, where they come complete with a novelty mug, dinner salad, and souvenir photo. Too good to be true, but too frequent to dismiss, you can't traverse Texas without being bombarded by these brightly colored come-ons. Mile after mile, they write checks your brain knows won't cash, but you keep driving toward the bank anyway.

But your stomach's got just one thing to do—eat—unless you're so fat that you can actually steer with it. Regardless, the stomach's got time

on its hands so its mind is bound to wander. The billboards know this. They also know the stomach, and possibly the unit, are the only organs dumb enough to believe a restaurant that gives away four and a half pound steaks all day could be profitable enough to finance a marketing campaign that rivals Nike's. The Big Texan billboards are physical proof you've left America and crossed over into the Republic of Texas.

I've been to the Big Texan twice, once for the show, and first in 1985 on my big drive to college. My roomie Rob and I stuffed my '78 powder-blue hand-me-down Malibu with our worldly possessions, took our highlighted AAA Chicago–L.A. map and $200 in cash, and set out on our Labor Day adventure: I-55 south out of Chicago, I-44 southwest out of St. Louis to Oklahoma City and the worst roadside Chinese food I've ever had, then into Texas on I-40.

Yes, my first romantic TDW was with a hairy Jewish guy from Long Island who thought he was Bruce Springsteen. Sadly, hard as we tried each night, the local ladies did not fully embrace our concept of romance. Instead we ended up alone in crappy motels, fighting over which channel to watch and drinking Mickey's Wide Mouth Malt Liquor.

But it was thrilling, our 1,700-mile joyride. We knew we were closing the coloring book on our childhoods and writing our first grown-up chapter. On Thursday, Rob and I both checked out of childhood and wouldn't rest until we'd settled onto our coed, ocean view dorm floor at UCLA on Monday night. That was our romance, youth's love affair with the world they know they will conquer.

As soon as we hit I-88, we rolled down the windows and Rob/Bruce belted out "Thunder Road." We were pulling outta there to win.

Except we lost, because $82 of our $200 nest egg was gone after our first stop at the Mississippi River Paddle Boats. Never play roulette on a boat. Bent, but not broken, we climbed back in the Blue Bomber and headed south. I was so depressed I didn't even see the first one whiz by outside Joplin. Soon, they started buzzing our brains like flies trapped in the back seat. Every ten miles we were teased by the Texans; eventually they took over.

"Getting hungry?" I asked Rob, just outside of OKC.

"Yeah. I'm craving steaks," he said.

At that moment, another one popped from behind a Stuckey's, framed against the pancake flat horizon like a cartoon house. I slowed down and for the first time, we really studied the incredible offer. The idea of a delicious FREE dinner got more appealing with every mile, until outside of Shamrock, Texas, it stopped being just an idea and gurgled into a scheme.

"Let's see . . . 72 ounces, that's four and a half pounds," I said, sounding like every pontificating fat ass that's ever stood around a Weber while someone else grilled the meat. "That's probably the pre-cooking weight . . . "

"Yeah. But only an idiot would eat four and a half pounds of meat . . . "

"And pay for it," I agreed. "But if it's free . . . "

"But if it's not," Rob moped, "we're screwed."

Another billboard whizzed by, this one advertising the shrimp cocktail included in the FREE dinner. Rob looked at me.

"We're pussies," he grimaced. Pause. "Let's do it."

I floored it and we sped off toward the Wizard of Seventy-two Oz.

The exterior of the Big Texan was, and still is, bright yellow. The vast parking lot is spitting distance from I-40, if ya got the

right kind of chew. The Big Texans embrace kitsch, celebrating the glutton in all of us with a photo-op in the parking lot. Even before you walk through the door, they've convinced you to grub more meat for dinner than most Africans eat in a lifetime. Even the pigs are bigger in Texas.

I remember it was crowded inside the Big Texan, the long waiting area lined with sample cuts of beef on ice. The legend of The Big Texan was posted on the wall to warn all who dare challenge the grill. But Rob and I were young, poor, and dumb enough not to be intimidated. Sure, only 16 percent of the people who tried actually finish the thing, but so what? Grannies did it. Kids did it. German tourists did it. Their smiling faces adorned the walls, proving to all who enter that it was possible! Why not us?

The last slab of meat in the case, the one right next to the host's podium, was The One we'd salivated over for miles. The "Big Texan" cut was the size of a Stephen King hardcover, but not quite as scary. I remember thinking that it didn't look like four and a half pounds, but then I wasn't a licensed rodeo clown, so what did I know? I quietly mentioned to the hostess that we were here for the free seventy-two-ounce steak dinners.

"Ain't you sweeeeeet," she smiled. "Are y'all sure you want to try? You know you gotta eat the whole meal in one hour to get it free. That's the seventytwoounce steak, baked potata, salad, shrimp cocktail, and bev'ridge a your choice. Otherwise it's $45 each. Plus tax and gratuity."

Altogether, we had $112 in our pockets and the billboards in our stomachs.

"We'll do it!"

An air raid horn ripped the quiet barn to shreds as servers bolted out of the kitchen, surrounding us like hungry cannibals.

They whisked us to a special table high above the suckers who were paying for their food, why I wasn't quite sure. We submitted our order, well done, and waited. Guys came up and wished us good luck. Moms pulled their kids away. Girls whispered as they walked by . . . we felt good.

The PA announcer interrupted the twangy music by announcing our names and encouraging the patrons to give us a hand. A team of waiters paraded out of the kitchen and ceremoniously dropped our meals on the table.

An air raid horn ripped the quiet barn to shreds as servers bolted out of the kitchen, surrounding us like hungry cannibals.

We'd been duped. The "sample" cut in the ice case was a ruse, maybe half the size of what sizzled before us. This real steak was literally the size of a Frisbee and folded over on itself, a double layer of meat at least three inches thick and fourteen inches across, scarier than Stephen King's entire library. I couldn't believe it—Texans had lied about size!

Now I understood why we were on a stage—sixty minutes of comic relief. For starters, because we'd had them char the meat beyond recognition, the ten-second chew estimate was way low. Our steaks were so dry it was like trying to chug jerky. Rob started with the extras, I tore into the meat, but thirty minutes into our hour we'd barely dented the cow. The bell rang after sixty minutes and we hung our heads as the MC laughed us off the stage.

Having no doubt faced many dine and dashers over the years, the three very Big Texans standing at the front doors

waved hello as our server dropped the $106 check. Not that it mattered; our bellies were so stuffed with beefy cement there'd be no way to outrun them without all kinds of messy complications. We paid the bill with a $1 tip, leaving us five bucks for the next one thousand miles.

"That's five cents every ten miles," mumbled Rob. "Doable."

Now that our pockets were empty, we took the opportunity to fill them with anything we could pilfer. Nauseous and chagrined, we clanked out to the parking lot with two horseshoe ashtrays, a glass cowboy boot mug, a napkin dispenser, and enough leftover steak to assemble our own calf. That, and this story, was all we had to sustain us until the Malibu pulled onto the UCLA campus forty hours later.

I had only one regret from that stomach-stretching day, and returning to the Big Texan two decades later for *Taste of America* gave me the chance to make things right. I needed to steal a matching mug.

One big glass cowboy boot was nice, but I needed a set . . . you know, for when I entertain. But evidently Rob and I hadn't been the only angry suckers who'd taken a souvenir over the years. The ornately carved glass mugs were all gone and had been replaced with cheap, purple plastic copies that wouldn't last one dishwasher cycle, let alone two decades of Texas tall tales. I ordered a regular ribeye and chuckled as two young dudes tried in vain to do the thing up on our stage. After their ritual humiliation was complete, I walked outside with my crappy purple cup.

The warm Texas air reminded me of my first trip through town, and I started thinking about all the TDW trips since, each with its own cast and character. TDWs can be the most romantic

My Favorite . . . CHAIN RESTAURANT
Waffle House, Everywhere in the South.
Literally.

There are over 1,500 Waffle Houses dotting the southern states, and if you were blindfolded and dropped into one, you'd have no idea which Waffle House you were in. Not that you'd care. They all have the same boxcar design, the same countertop, littered with ashtrays and elbows, the same jukebox filled with southern rock and a few Waffle House anthems.

COURTESY OF WAFFLE HOUSE INC.

In the Waffle House, you don't have to ask for more coffee, you beg them to stop. THAT'S service. The coffee delivers a jolt like a defibrillator, though it's probably more the heavy ceramic cups, endless pot, and the broads who pour it, than the beans.

That . . . and the swirling cigarette smoke of the four hundred pound trucker hunkered on the next stool, using your toast as an ashtray.

In Hollywood, being a waitress is a temporary penance hot girls pay until they become starlets. In a Waffle House, being a waitress is what hot girls do after retiring from the pageant circuit and before joining the Red Hat Ladies.

Even better than breakfast, though, is nightcapping at the Waffle House. Nightcapping happens after the bars close, but before the southern sunrise: the hours when their jukeboxes play "Freebird" on a continual loop, with occasional drops of "Grill Operator/Waffle House," and "Waffle House for You and Me—instrumental." When one of your friends achieves Drungry—the perfect balance of drunk and hungry—and orders two chili-cheese omelets, it's time to wobble out to the parking lot and clear the drop zone. These are the hours made for YouTube.

COURTESY OF WAFFLE HOUSE INC.

memories to make, especially if you're headed to an event designed for good times, someplace like a festival.

All festivals look good on paper, but do your research before you commit a precious TDW. You don't want to drive all the way to Circleville's Pumpkin Festival if you don't love gourds. It's a great small town celebration, but really, if squash and pumpkins don't FASCINATE you, don't burn the gas just to see zucchini shaped like Lincoln and Jefferson. But if you do go, make sure you stick around until they bring out the Big Ones for the Largest Pumpkin Contest. The year we visited, the winning pumpkin weighed 1,350 pounds, but as a result of the chemicals used to grow it, couldn't be eaten. Can't get more American than that— even our champion pumpkins are on the juice.

Who you meet at festivals has more effect on your overall enjoyment than where you are and what you do. When we went to Indianapolis for the Strawberry Shortcake Festival, the Cathedral Women gave us a VIP tour of downtown and we got great shots of the State Soldiers' and Sailors' Monument. We also met some very interesting people—the FBI.

It was early June and kids that had spent the last nine months locked up in school were running wild, pelting each other with water balloons and squirt guns. The fountains were bubbling at full force and the line for free strawberry shortcakes snaked all the way around the monument. But we had VIP credentials, which meant we could get into the white tent for cold beverages and dessert whenever we felt like it. Power like that is only wielded in banana republics and countries too difficult to name here because of their spelling, so we took full advantage.

The Cathedral Women had an assembly line set up in the basement. Some sliced the berries, some scooped the whipped cream, others baked the shortbread, a far cry from the way they were made when the Native Americans introduced the colonists to their delicious corn and strawberry "bread." The collision of sweet, juicy strawberries and cool non-dairy whipped topping with the crunchy shortbread has evolved into the perfect hot weather dessert. Over four decades ago, these Indianapolis women laid claim to the best in the country, and after having a few, I was convinced they were right.

The problem was people were eating them so fast we couldn't get any good video. It was late in the day and we still needed some energetic footage of people enjoying their strawberry shortcakes. That's when I came up with the bright idea of a contest. I gathered a few of the more outlandish-looking guys around and issued a challenge: Whoever could perform the most outrageous or hilarious stunt on or around the monument's fountain could skip the long shortcake line and get into the cool basement with us.

A couple guys sang songs, another did a headstand next to a statue, but frankly we weren't impressed. I told the last guy perhaps he

COURTESY OF BRIAN MILLER

might have a better chance of winning if he ended up IN the fountain instead of dancing around it. We rolled tape and the guy leapt into the water, splashing and screaming like an angry marlin. Instant winner.

And instant trouble. Out of nowhere, guys in suits and sunglasses materialized and grabbed him like he was Jack Ruby. They flashed badges in the kid's face, and without skipping a beat he pointed directly at me. I told Brian to keep rolling as they charged me. The biggest guy shoved his badge in my face.

"FBI. What the hell are you doing?" he demanded.

I had never seen an FBI badge before. For the record, they clinch your butt faster than a big sneeze.

"You're trespassing on federal property. That's a felony!" he growled.

"We were just . . . ," I began.

"I got eyes," the G-man barked. "We've got thousands of people surrounding this monument, a potential terrorism target, and you are inciting defacement and trespass. Do you know what that means?"

I'm thinking, this is gonna be a GREAT segment! But what I said was, "No, sir."

"That's not a lap pool. It's part of a monument to soldiers and sailors that died protecting this country, and you're making a mockery of them."

"I . . . I . . . " I was speechless, "wasn't making a mockery . . . "

"Enticing someone to do the backstroke while holding a balloon between his legs isn't mocking?"

"Well . . . "

"You've got two options," the FBI officer said. "Cease and desist, surrender your tape and walk away, or keep arguing."

And now you know why you never saw any of this on the show. I don't scare easily, but those badges clinched me up pretty good. Afterwards, I took the time to really look at the monument. I almost threw up out of shame.

Plaques on each of the four sides are dedicated to local men and women of the four service branches who'd fought and died for our country. The FBI was right, by goofing off ON the monument, it looked like we were making fun of it. Nothing romantic about being an asshole with a camera. I felt horrible, then relieved that no one in our office would ever see the tape. Every few years I do something so stupid, it stuns even me.

THAT'S why you research before you go to your festival. No matter what your interest or hobby, somewhere in America someone is organizing a festival for it. These are all real festivals. Really:

Mr. & Mrs. Cat Universe Pageant
www.pageantuniversity.com/catu2007

Civil War Re-enactor Competition
www.crystalriverreenactment.org/livefire_reg.html

Redneck Olympics
www.2camels.com/videos/redneck-games.php

National Karaoke Championships
www.talentqst.com/

Land & Sea Kinetic Sculpture Race
www.kineticbaltimore.com/

Clowning World Championships
www.coai.org/competition_rules.htm

National Magic Competition
www.daytonamagic.com/

Knock yourself out.

Depending on who and where you are, the events above can all be romantic TDWs, but there is one destination that for almost one hundred years has nurtured lovers of all kinds, a place of pastoral grace, pungent flavors, and toe-curling excitement. Five generations have fallen in love here and kept the documentation to prove it. If "love" is that spark, that instant and eternal connection, then this is its temple: Wrigley Field.

Wrigley Field is the most romantic destination in America. It's the perfect TDW because it's in the middle of America and is a place where magic almost happens every day of the home schedule. If your mate doesn't know or love Wrigley, dump them.

Wrigley Field is a mystical vortex. Shit happens within those brick walls that simply couldn't in the real world: The Collapse, the Black Cat, The Goat. . . . Wrigley fans, by virtue of their intimacy with both elation and soul-crushing heartbreak, develop a unique empathy for the human condition not found anywhere else in the known universe. That sensitivity is essential to any romantic relationship. No macho guy would ever admit this, and no girl would ever conceive it, but it's true.

The park—and it is a park, not a stadium or a facility—is nestled in a neighborhood of brownstones and businesses. Bars and iconic restaurants ring the dowager queen like petticoats, providing a game day buzz that starts humming before dawn and burns long after dark. At Wrigley Field a three-hour ballgame lasts at least twelve. It's the perfect first date. You can wine and dine, watch the game, then dance the night away. Or take indoor batting practice at Sluggers; either way, you'll never run out of things to talk about.

> Wrigley fans, by virtue of their intimacy with both elation and soul-crushing heartbreak, develop a unique empathy for the human condition not found anywhere else in the known universe.

If it's your first trip to Wrigley, arrive two hours early and do whatcha gotta do to buy a bleacher seat. Yes, there are better seats in the park, better if you're a professional scout and are charting pitches. But there is no better place in the park, the city of Chicago, or perhaps all of America to meet interesting people than the bleachers. The fun starts the moment the green iron gates at the corner of Waveland and Sheffield swing open to release the thundering general admission horde into the skeleton of the famous scoreboard. Scrambling up the gum-pocked cement ramps in the dark, the grail of first-row seats hangs in the balance. But before the dash to "your spot," there is always the moment when you walk up out of the darkness and into the Wrigley sunshine. That light is the mythical "brilliant light," the near-death people talk about. Good moment for a kiss, but keep it moving or you'll be instantly trampled and experience it for real.

The bleachers have their own food service. Don't leave until you've had a "Beef," some Old Styles, peanuts of course, then top it all off with a Frosty Malt, a scoopable semi-frozen delight that will leave you sticky for a week. For ballpark food, Wrigley sets the standard. No sushi, no buffalo . . . if Babe Ruth never ate it, neither should you. Beer etiquette demands that you stack your empty cups in your aisle as you drink, thereby giving ushers and fellow fans a graphic index of your level of intoxication.

So grab your date and watch them watch Wrigley. In a world where nothing ever stays the same, Wrigley Field is an oasis of splendor. And anyone who appreciates that is a lover worth keeping. Someone more entranced by experience than outcome. A partner who insists on monogamy, fidelity, and unconditional love regardless of logic. And above all, someone who'll share those experiences with you because your very presence makes them better.

PHOTO BY KEN CARL

Which is what the romance of the Three-Day Weekend is all about. Hitting "pause" to escape to a place where nothing is more important than a silly game, or giant pumpkin, or a fancy rat.

A weekend where the players are more important than the final score.

STRAWBERRY SHORTCAKE RECIPE

The ladies at the Strawberry Shortcake Festival in Indianapolis say they cannot reveal the intricate details of their delicious recipe. So after eating several, I thought I'd take a stab at it:

Combine strawberries that have been sitting in their own juice overnight with square shortbread slices and whipped topping. You can also add in ice cream if it's especially warm.

Place in paper bowl and consume quickly using plastic forks while searching for shade.

At least that's what I remember.

Chapter 14
Heading Home

All I remember about being a kid is that it took too long. Holidays were the worst because I'd always get stuck at the kiddie table with the dribblers. All the action was at the grownup table; the whispered secrets punctuated by bawdy laughter sounded like so much fun compared to pushing peas around my Yogi Bear plate. The louder the old Italians got, the more I'd beg to move up. But not until my much younger fifth cousin was old enough to sit upright did I get my promotion.

Cookie and the other aunts—Juanna, Lena, Lucy, Gingie, Mels, Toots, Rosie, Marilyn, and Silvia the Nut—taught me the rhythm of conversation, and how to really listen . . . because sometimes what people don't say speaks the loudest.

Cookie also taught me about secrets, "If people know you won't tell anything, they'll tell you everything." Turns out she was right. The stories and secrets I've heard in Beale Street blues clubs, at Ritz-Carlton cocktail parties, and behind Little League backstops are more entertaining and scandalous than any "reality" show could ever invent. Most of my interesting facts and figures can be traced back to those loud laughfests around a kitchen table.

They all came in handy on Friday, March 22. Specifically, the March three months after I graduated, flat broke, from UCLA and won over $115,000 on NBC's *Sale of the Century* game show. I didn't have to eat lizard colon or convince my family I was marrying a gay circus midget with Tourette's syndrome. I just answered questions using the previously useless knowledge the aunts and others stuck in my head, and as a result, became the show's all-time champion. I also won a fire engine red convertible upon which I affixed the first and only vanity plate I will ever own: CHMPYN.

On that lucky day, I vowed that I would drive that car, that I'd use those fantastic free wheels to see America one Waffle House at a time. I vowed that each year, on or about March 22, I'd get out of L.A. and take a solo road trip someplace I had never been, someplace new, because even as a freshly minted college graduate, I knew I didn't know squat. I also thought it'd be entertaining to be reminded that not everyone in America is tan, thin, and "almost finished with a totally awesome screenplay."

So each spring until 1992, I climbed into CHMPYN all by myself and took off for two weeks of comedy gigs, eccentric people, and fascinating places. I didn't use guidebooks—too obvious, or GPS—too un-invented yet, just curiosity and the desire to assemble the greatest collection of stolen motel towels of anyone I knew.

I traveled alone to force myself to really meet the people I met. I learned the stranger they are, the more they like to

talk, especially when the stranger senses you're actually interested in what they have to say. All my years apprenticing at The Aunts table provided me with the skills to draw ridiculous stories out of perfect strangers. When a woman you've known for literally four minutes can be con-

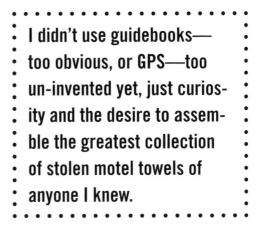

I didn't use guidebooks—too obvious, or GPS—too un-invented yet, just curiosity and the desire to assemble the greatest collection of stolen motel towels of anyone I knew.

vinced to remove her artificial leg and pound it on the bullet-proof Texaco window until they open their bathroom at 4:00 a.m., you know you're in the zone.

Traveling alone forced me to listen. One night west of Sidney, Nebraska, I heard the sound of midnight love on my CB. "Annie Q" was driving I-80 on a new route, and wanted to know the best place to grub 'n' scrub before Cheyenne. "Pepper Jack" breakered back that the twenty-four-hour chili up ahead at the Highway 212 exit was Texas good, and he oughta know because he was from Texas. Annie Q couldn't believe it. She grew up in Texas City, right across Galveston Bay. For the next eighty miles, I was a fly in the cab on their first date. They talked about everything: weigh stations, tires, the Astros. Annie deftly worked in how her ex didn't understand her love of the road. PJ told her that it took a special kind of woman to make the entire country her home, the same kind, ironically, that could appreciate a good Texas chili. Then he asked her to dinner—over the air. And she said yes!

"I'll go on up ahead to 212 and get us a table," squelched Pepper. "How'll I know you?"

"I'm a tattooed blonde in a Roadway Peterbilt," she squawked.
"10-4" was all he said.

As I spun off the ramp at 212 and drove through truck parking, I was relieved to see I'd beaten the Peterbilt. I parked my car in the amateur lot and scrambled into the diner, anxious to see the show. The counter was packed with big, sweaty guys in torn caps, loose jeans, and more man-cleavage than a plumber's yoga class. Not particularly appetizing at 1:00 a.m., but I wasn't here to eat.

Empty Formica tables dotted the diner all the way to the corner where a heavy-set hoss in a cowboy hat sat, holding a blinking plastic rose. Unlike his comrades, his face was freshly scrubbed, and the hands fidgeting with his silverware were clean enough to eat with. Every time a truck roared into the parking lot he peeked from underneath his Stetson, then went back to fidgeting. We sat there a long time, me watching him watch the window.

After thirty minutes of constant flashing, the battery in the rose finally died. We'd been stood up. Jack looked down and began tinkering with his flower. As he did, a middle-aged, inked-up blondie slipped into the diner.

She'd obviously stopped to "freshen up." Her blue eye shadow sparkled in the harsh light from the rotating pie case and the fold marks on her Metallica t-shirt were visible from across the diner, but Jack was too busy trying to fix her flower to notice.

She stopped at the hostess desk and scanned the room. In a flash, a buffed-up bald guy jumped up from the counter cradling a bag.

"Annie?" Baldy made sure to speak softly so none of the other truckers could hear him. "I got us complete chili dinners to go . . . I got video in my cab. Have you seen *Point Break*?"

"I love Patrick Swayze!" Annie said as Baldy spun her away from the room and back toward the door. "Did you pack enough hot sauce?" she smiled. Baldy held the door and Annie walked through it.

The real Pepper Jack was still fixated on his electronic gardening when I broke the Prime Directive.

"Pepper Jack!"

Baldy didn't stop, but Annie spun her head back toward my voice at the exact instant Pepper Jack turned toward the restaurant. Neither of them saw me, but it didn't matter. Annie stopped in her tracks and stared. Across the diner, Pepper Jack stood and offered her a burned-out plastic rose.

"It's good chili . . . ," Baldy stammered.

In a blur, Annie grabbed the paper bag containing two relatively fragile Styrofoam containers of steaming, truck stop chili, and slammed it down on Baldy's dome.

The splat! echoed through the suddenly silent diner. Out on the highway, a truck horn punctuated the glop like a silent movie sound effect.

"You are a piece of shit!" she screamed as the heavy door smacked Baldy's sizzling scalp. Annie stepped over his crumpled body, back into the diner. The

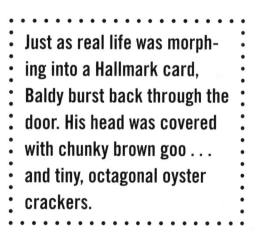

Just as real life was morphing into a Hallmark card, Baldy burst back through the door. His head was covered with chunky brown goo . . . and tiny, octagonal oyster crackers.

truckers stared in silence as the real Jack walked across the diner and handed Annie her rose.

Just as real life was morphing into a Hallmark card, Baldy burst back through the door. His head was covered with chunky brown goo . . . and tiny, octagonal oyster crackers.

As the counter choir's hysterical laughter bounced off the stainless steel grill hoods, the Biggest Trucker blocked the doorway.

"YOU are a BOWL of shit," he said, blocking Baldy's charge. "Go wipe . . . and don't come back."

Pepper Jack and Annie watched through their corner booth window as Baldy's gas tanker groaned its way out of the parking lot. By the time Annie turned back to the table, the waitress had slipped a real red carnation into her water glass. And with that, we all returned to our business, leaving them to whatever fate had planned.

All the world really is a stage. And for two weeks every year, I made sure I had a front seat.

But all good things come to an end. In 1992, after eight glorious years, my solo ramblings came screeching to a halt when I opened up a birthday box and found a puppy. But not just any puppy: my first pet, of any kind, ever.

Groucho and I did everything together. He slept on a pillow beside me, ate his dinners at my feet, and chilled out in every dressing room I've ever had. For his first birthday, Aunt Cookie sent me a hardcover of my favorite book—*Travels with Charley*. Stealing Steinbeck's idea, the following year I rechristened my spring trips "birthday" trips, and for the next twelve years Groucho and I traveled the country with the top down and our eyes open.

So it was that I was already a seasoned traveler when the Travel Channel tapped me to host *Taste of America* in October of 2004. After a decade roaming with my rover I'd become uniquely qualified to enjoy the ultimate synergy—turning my bliss into my paycheck. My only problem was Groucho—my new travel schedule would keep us apart for months at a time, unless I could figure out a clever solution.

I remember waking up that day, a week before our first road shoot, with his snout inches from mine. Groucho was breathing fast and his legs were twitching like an Arabian. His eyes popped open and he immediately looked disappointed: no squirrel, just me.

I rubbed his belly and got up to make coffee. Groucho stretched and yawned like a Tex Avery cartoon. With the clang of treats in his bowl, I heard him flop off the bed and patter toward the kitchen. He walked out into the living room and dropped the treats on the carpet while staring at the birds chirping outside the window. Then he jumped on the treats and chomped them to bits. I was going to miss our morning ritual.

By noon Groucho was snoring on his rug, sprawled in the sunlight coming through the French door. I had to leave for a photo shoot, but a friend was coming over to take him on his favorite walk. Nearby Runyon Canyon was a wonderland filled with birds, squirrels, joggers, waterfalls, and a menagerie of dogs and their equally eccentric owners. But my friend was late, so I left her a key and sat down on the couch to tie my shoes.

Silently, I thought "Groucho" and stared at him. At that instant, his eyes slid open as his head wobbled up and he looked right at me.

It startled me. Not because he heard me think his name; we did that all the time. But because his eyes were red and cloudy. He looked tired. Very, very tired. For an instant I was scared. Then, I laughed. He always looked so funny when he woke up. I laughed louder because I knew in just minutes she'd show up and he'd be jumping around with his leash in his mouth. I laughed because I knew the future. Then I went to the door and walked out.

I'd known for a while he was slowing down. His Frisbee jumps weren't spectacular anymore; sometimes he even missed. It took fewer tosses to get him to take the tennis ball in his gray muzzle and go home. I knew the clock was ticking, but always assumed we'd have ample warning, time to sit and just hold onto each other.

And we did. I just didn't use it. I laughed . . . and left.

Even in death he was a good dog. On a walk in his favorite canyon, he just sat down and quietly left. No screeching of tires. No needle administered in anguish. His heart was just tired. The same heart that beat like a snare drum in his sink bath twelve years before. He even told me it was time, but I was already late.

Her frantic call. A dash across town to the vet. Too late.

It was really late by the time I climbed the steps to my front door in silence. I opened the door unmolested. I fell onto my bed . . . alone. Eventually I woke up and hit the road with no need to look back.

In time, the days got brighter and I embraced my new job as if it were an old friend. I used to roll down the road recapping a particularly entertaining day to a dog; now I did it to a cam-

era. Outside of looking less crazy at stoplights, I assumed my exploits would be more review than revelation.

I was wrong.

Groucho never met Paula April and her Red Hat Ladies. If we'd ever gotten down to Mobile, Alabama, just one bite of Paula's bourbon-soaked bread pudding would have laid him out. He was more partial to spilled beer than bourbon.

In L.A., the fun girls go to clubs. In the South, they belong to clubs. The Red Hat Ladies are a group of boisterous dames who've worked their way up through Brownies, Girl Scouts, Pom-Poms, cheerleading, sororities, ladies auxiliary, den mother, and sports mom to "attain the age of 50." They may be on the back-side of one hundred, but that doesn't mean they're done throwing down, southern style. I know this because I spent an afternoon as their boy-toy.

Paula's house was filled with six elegant southern belles adorned in red hats, purple clothes, and high heels. They were making a bread pudding oozing with so much southern grace and bourbon we could have used it as a candle. Not that we needed one. Paula is a collector. Of everything. Figurines, statuettes, commemorative candles: animal, mineral, or unicorn, if

COURTESY OF PAULA APRIL

it's sold on late-night TV, Paula has a matching set displayed in her charming home. Every wall was lined with shelves from floor to ceiling, and every shelf was lovingly stocked with thangs. I would guess that the actual retail price of the items in Paula's house exceeded the value of the house. She gave me an exhaustive tour of her collection while the bread pudding baked and the Ladies sipped the leftover bourbon. By the time the pudding was ready, I needed the booze too.

Paula served up the delicious bourbon-soaked pudding on her finest china while we sipped tea and chatted like ladies of distinction. Then the bourbon soaked into us. A quick poll of the couch revealed that all the gentlewomen owned and operated purple undergarments of some kind. Much to my relief, ladies of "a certain age" still like to wear sexy underwear, as long as it's Red Hat approved. Knowing naughty survives middle age is life affirming, and gives me something more to look forward to than just a discount on movie tickets. I wrapped up the segment and spent the next hour talking naughty with the grannies. Days like the Red Hat Afternoon are the reasons I love the South. We're a country of sexy septuagenarian broads.

Next we went to Little Rock to party with the Maverick Mixers, a group of socialite seniors who gather once a month to eat a square meal and do a square dance. Sweet Gwen McKim, who along with Gerald, her husband of fifty-one years, leads the Mixers, introduced me to two southern delicacies in one night.

Most southern food rose from the ashes of necessity. Inventive cooks took what they could find and did their best to make it palatable. Usually, that meant deep-frying. Everything.

Farms and plantations always had plenty of fat to melt down into grease. They learned that by adding flour and egg—also in plentiful supply—to whatever scraps they had could feed more people after frying. They started with chicken and continued working down the food chain until they'd used every vegetable that fit in the frying pan.

This combination of impatience and hunger eventually yielded a southern staple. Green tomatoes are just unripe regular red tomatoes that are picked because of their tart taste and firm consistency. Around Little Rock, nobody made better fried green tomatoes than Gwen the Maverick.

After shopping for the perfect fruit—yes, they're fruits—Gwen drove me over to the American Legion hut to start the festivities. While her square dancers set up the same record player you remember from sixth grade filmstrips, Gwen led me into the Legion's tiny kitchen where a cast iron skillet was bubbling with oil. We mixed up some flour, egg, and spices, dipped the tomato slices, and fried 'em up. That was the extent of Gwen's family recipe. Simple, but delicious, especially after a hard night of dancing the original hip-hop.

Gerald and Gwen started throwing these parties fifteen years ago because "they're a good, clean activity—no drinking, smoking, or cussing." They found that people were starving afterwards, but had nowhere to eat since all the local restaurants were closed. That's when the social director added "chef" to her "to do" list.

Ever since, the monthly meetings of the Maverick Mixers have been THE social events in the county. Once we'd fried up our bag of tomatoes, we headed out to the dance floor to revisit my grade school nightmare.

In addition to giving the Anti-Christ a run for his/her money, my eighth grade warden Sister Margaret Jean loved square dancing, probably because all her students hated it. She loved it so much, she forced the P.E. teacher at St. Joseph's grade school to include a four-week square dance module as a graduation requirement. Every Friday in December we went down to the basement and lined up boys against the bleachers, girls against the stage. Then she put the record on the turntable and forced us to pick a date and stumble around a painted circle for a square dance. I'd hated it then, and I hadn't really missed it since. But Gwen assured me that tonight would be nothin' but fun. How could I doubt a grandmother in a poodle skirt? We watched for a few dances, then Gwen grabbed the microphone.

"Ladies," she drawled, "we got us a new dancer tonight. Let's show him what the Maverick Mixers is all about!"

The record whirred to life, swarming me with seventy-year-old belles in frilly, button-covered outfits. I may be the worst dancer on two legs, but that didn't stop the grannies. They passed me around their circle like the cable guy in a sorority house, bumping and grinding and swooshing, while their grumpy husbands watched from the bar. The Maverick Mixettes were patient and hands-on . . . very. Must be something in the fried green tomatoes.

As the dancing continued, the guys who'd been husbands longer than I'd been alive began to circle our square. And when the Conway Twitty slow song came on, they started square-blocking me. We'd only get in one or two "swing your partners" before they'd dance their wives away. One of 'em stood in front of the exit, like I was going to waltz his Matilda out the door. Eventually, I realized the ladies were vamping me on purpose just to rile up their men! The dancin' grannies used me like a piece of deep-fried southern meat . . . and I liked it. We're a country of jealous geezers.

It was 8:00 a.m. in Jackson Hole, Wyoming, and I needed some coffee before heading off to the Pinedale Rodeo Grounds for something called pitchfork fondue.

Darrell Walker loved fondue, but couldn't stand how long it took to do the beef cube by cube. In typical cowboy fashion, he insisted on inventing a way to fondue an entire T-bone at a time. His answer: one fifty-five-gallon drum filled with boiling oil and a pitchfork loaded with twelve to fifteen steaks. All summer long, Darrell and his lovely wife Verna fed hungry carnivores at their dip, sizzle, and serve Rodeo Grounds cowboy feasts.

But the grounds were two hours away, which is why I was up extra early and sitting in the hotel lounge while Fox News oozed its slime from the TV. Even though we were in cattle country, it was more bullshit than I could take at that hour, so I turned the TV to CNN.

"What the hell?" bellowed a cowboy hidden back in the corner. "I was watching the news."

"No . . . you weren't," I said, just hung over enough to pick a fight. "That was Fox. Everything they just said is factually, morally, and demonstrably wrong. They invent it to rile up reactionary idiots."

The rancher jumped up and screamed, "Who you callin' idiots?"

"I'm sorry, I didn't see you sitting there," I explained. "But really, watching that crap is a waste of time. You won't get any real news. Why don't we . . . "

He stood eight inches taller than me and narrowed his eyes. "You're one of them Hollywood liberals, ain't you?"

Typical. Just because we disagreed, this shitkicker's first impulse was to insult me and label me as an ignorant anti-American. Which, truth be told, is exactly what I'd done to him, except I hadn't said it out loud. Luckily my crew arrived and extricated me like a S.W.A.T. team. We are a country of polar opposites who can't agree on polar ice caps, or polar bears.

I was still fuming when we got to the Rodeo Grounds. Darrell and Verna had invited twenty of their cowboy and cowgirl friends and family to share our feast. After we cooked his delicious potato chips, the oil was hot enough to fondue the steaks. Darrell took a regular pitchfork, one he only used for cooking he hastily pointed out, and speared four T-bone steaks onto each tine. After all twelve were locked and loaded, Darrell simply stuck the pitchfork into the boiling oil.

Sssssssssssssssssss! It was like a scene out of a Bond film. The meat sizzled . . . like raw meat in hot oil. According to Darrell, the intense heat immediately seared the outside of the meat, sealing in the flavor and cooking it in seconds, not minutes. Far from turning out greasy or "fried," the steaks were juicy and tender and had everyone licking their chops for seconds. He even had a system for cooking rare and well done on the same pitchfork. First, he plunged in the entire tool, then after a few moments, twisted the handle to elevate one of the tines out of the oil. The meat continued to cook itself, but at a slow enough rate that by the time the submerged steaks were done, the others were still red and bleeding.

"Now THAT'S fondue," Darrell grinned. "None of that itsy, bitsy cubes. You die of starvation eating a meal that slow . . . this is Cowboy Fondue."

Judging from the happy faces and empty plates, I'd have to agree with my new pardner. As we sat at the long picnic tables finishing up dessert, one of the cowboys asked me where we were staying, and I told the story of my morning battle. As I looked around the grounds, I realized I was probably telling the wrong story to the wrong people, but I'd gone too far to stop now. I finished up my tale of our confrontation, and tried to change the subject. That's when Jerry, the biggest rancher at the dinner cleared his throat. I saw Brian reach for our truck keys.

Jerry's boots were caked with mud and he wore a cowboy hat because it worked, not because it looked good hanging in his corner office. I braced for another withering attack as Jerry pointed at me and unloaded his wisdom.

"People are ignorant," he growled. "Just because a guy comes from Hollywood or wears silly shirts, don't mean you know anything about the man."

My shirt was silly?

That got everyone at the long table talking, and soon it was a full-blown debate. I'm embarrassed to admit that I was shocked to find both sides represented. Sure, plenty of these folks watched Fox News, but

We talked Liberty, Democracy, and Freedom while the sun set majestically behind the purple mountains. All we needed was Ray Charles and his Fabulous Raylettes. We're a country where the patriots don't all wear the same hats.

they explained the rancher problems in ways I'd never heard on CNN. Perhaps it was the calming influence of twenty ounces of

steak in our stomachs, but what unfolded during the next hour was a loud, funny, and reasonable discussion, Red and Blue playing nice, out on the range. By dusk, I had learned a lot about land management, our food chain, and all the work and risk it takes to put a steak on the table, fondued or not.

We talked Liberty, Democracy, and Freedom while the sun set majestically behind the purple mountains. All we needed was Ray Charles and his Fabulous Raylettes. We're a country where the patriots don't all wear the same hats.

After three weeks in the frozen North, I landed in Miami to shoot the last episode of the show. It had been several years since I faced the terror of those forty-two bridges to bask in the pinks and blues of Mallory Square. I'd visited four hundred cities since I began the journey that would end hours later under that same sunset.

As we drove away from MIA, down the palm-lined streets of South Beach, I started thinking about my expectations on that first flight to Key West, so many months before. My cocky belief that this show would be just a familiar trip back to the iconic places I already knew, the sense that I'd already met every possible iteration of *American*. I laughed out loud realizing how wrong I'd been.

True, mini-malls, outlet malls, and mega-malls maul the landscape like retail pimples. Yes, the Web manifests the far-flung at our fingertips in nano-seconds. And cable TV now has a channel for everyone: animals, agnostics, blacks, boomers, buffs, gays, goalies, government, nerds, nuns, nuts . . . there's even GTV, God Television. The problem, as I see it anyway, is

My Favorite . . . BEACH
Miami

Sure, there are a lot more tropical places in the fifty states. Yes there are more mellow places to lounge in the sand, but Miami has it all.

Hot Latin culture, music and clubs for nighttime, and warm, sunny, crowded beaches during the day—Cuba Libre's flow freely on the sands at the high-end hotels, and even the pools feel like the beach.

And you can start every day with high octane Cuban coffee to make sure you don't miss a thread of the string bikinis that are all the rage these days. Thank God!

With the eclectic mix of cultures, it's almost like you're in a foreign country that takes our money—best of both worlds. The combination of the warm water, white sands, and hot beach-lovers make Miami the beachiest.

that too many people settle for these digital surrogates, rather than immersing themselves in the real thing. Millions of us are *watching* shadows instead of *casting* them.

Dull, yet ironically opinionated, these drones clog the landscape, gathering in self-satisfied clusters from sea to digitally enhanced sea, consuming franchise food, watching franchised reality, living franchised lives. But they aren't US.

US is all our tribes, not just the ones who grab the headlines and line up at Walmart in fantastic outfits. With 300 million of anything, there's bound to be quality control issues. Categorizing

"America" as any one thing is like trying to explain a raindrop by watching a fire hydrant blast kids on a summer street. But if you've read this far—not just starting here to find out who the killer is—you now know that the flame of individuality still flickers proudly in our Land.

So after eating my way across fifty states, D.C., and P.R., I'm happy to confirm that reports of the death of our culture are greatly exaggerated. Bent, but not irreversibly broken, we remain as weird, vibrant, and unpredictable as ever. Genuinely interesting and endearing people still thrive, they just don't come knocking on your door anymore. You've gotta make the effort.

> I'm happy to confirm that reports of the death of our culture are greatly exaggerated. Bent, but not irreversibly broken, we remain as weird, vibrant, and unpredictable as ever.

The Golden Gate Bridge spans the Bay every day, but nothing you see on television compares to actually walking across it yourself. And through four hundred cities, I did a lot of walking. Some things I experienced were shameful, others so uplifting that they seemed almost invented. And the last day of my cross-country expedition somehow magically encapsulated all of it, catching me totally by surprise.

I met Jorge Castillo early in that morning at Maximo Gomez Park. We both were sporting yellow island shirts, probably purchased at the same store. Evidently matching clothing is very emotional for the Cuban people, because the guy hugged me like a giant carnival prize the moment we met. Jorge looks like a cross between Andy Garcia and Nathan Lane and has the personality of a proud Cuban rush chairman.

He took me by the hand and started explaining every statue in the park. By the third one, he sensed my fatigue.

"We have much to do today," he bellowed. "But first—Cuban coffee in Domino Park!"

I had never tasted Cuban coffee before, but how different could it be from all the other ethnic javas? Never one to turn down an early morning zap of caffeine, I followed Jorge down a cobblestone sidewalk back into the park jammed with wrinkled Cubans to get my fix.

"Domino Park" sits in the heart of Little Havana and is always filled with boisterous, retired Cubans playing dominoes. These geezers drink, gamble, and scream all day long, stopping only long enough to mix their stones, or pass one.

I was instantly at home in this foreign place. I grew up around loud and energetic tables of old people: mine were women and they cooked; these were men and they smoked. Aside from that, they were identical. I felt like I was back in Chicago, stealing sips of beer out of Aunt Gingie's frosted Old Style mug.

The cackles of laughter with every defeat, the authoritative clank of a victorious domino being slammed into place, everything about Domino Park reminded me of home. Except I had no idea what they were saying. But I knew it was fun.

Jorge led me through the park and back to the street. He couldn't wait to introduce me to his coffee. We walked up to a street cart and he ordered two doubles. After a few minutes, a tiny Cuban woman stuck her shaky hand through the ripped screen cradling the steamy drinks. I started to add milk until Jorge screamed.

"No! First you must try it as it is."

I was clearly outnumbered, so I lifted the cup to my lips, then he screamed again.

"No! You need sucre! Agave nectar is also acceptable. Try it."

With that, he poured a metric ton of granulated sugar into my demitasse concoction.

"Now you can drink."

And I did. I don't know the Spanish word for heaven, but I know what it tastes like. Cuban coffee is brash and biting. I needed the sugar to keep my head from exploding. Jorge's toothy grin was almost as sweet as he proudly watched me enjoy his drink. I sat at the stand and savored every last drop as the fervor of the domino games continued to escalate.

I felt a rush of energy blow through my brain when I tried to stand up. Jorge just laughed.

> **It tasted like where angels go when they die and leave heaven. The physical experience of drinking that piping nectar calmed my soul and energized my body.**

"Now, some café con leche!" He waved imperially to the woman and she went back to work. This time, creating the same drink, but with the milk I was going to add in the first place. But not just any milk—steamed condensed milk, mixed perfectly into the espresso. I took my second first sip. It tasted like where angels go when they die and leave heaven. The physical experience of drinking that piping nectar calmed my soul and energized my body.

Jorge walked me through all the tables in the park, introducing me to a steady stream of grinning grandpas who had never seen our show. Nothing could interest them less, but they politely nodded and smiled, until we let them get back to business—dominoes.

Today we were making Cuban tamales from scratch with Jorge and his two partners, the "Three Guys from Miami." Jorge took me shopping for all the ingredients: corn husks, corn, meat, vegetables, and spices, then back to his house where we'd meet the other two "Guys," Raul and Glenn, and cook our feast.

After a forty-five-minute ride, we pulled into Jorge's driveway and my baptism began. Glenn and Raul met us in the kitchen and immediately started working on the tamales.

Raul Musibay is clearly Cuban. He looks, smells, dresses, and cooks Cuban. He arrived via Spain in 1980 and has called Miami his home since then. His thick accent sounds like rice and beans, and his cigar cologne completes the package. No problem.

Glenn Lindgren—big problem. "Gringo" doesn't do Glenn justice. Originally from Minnesota, home of Queen Ivey's lutefisk, alabaster-skinned Glenn came to Florida in 1983 and fell in love with the culture and the cuisine. He's the Guy who actually writes their cookbooks and can cook virtually any ethnic cuisine you can Google, from "American" to "Vietnamese." He doesn't speak Spanish, doesn't look Cuban, but doesn't act Lindgren. I thought I was being punked, and the real Third Guy would emerge from behind a palm tree and start laughing like Ricky Ricardo at any moment. But Glenn is no joke.

Three Guys from Miami are serious about their food—and even more serious about their fun.

"You've never had these before," declared Raul in his raspy, rum-soaked baritone. "The Mexican tamales that you get in restaurants around here, they're not handmade. We make ours from scratch. It takes a long time, but we have fun."

The first step was to take boiled corn on the cob and grate the kernels off with a cheese grater. After that, the pulp is cooked with spices and meat until it's like a porridge, then The Guys scoop the goop into the corn husks and tie them up like Cuban Christmas presents to cook them some more. Like so many of the ethnic foods I'd enjoyed during my four hundred city romp, tamales began as a way to stretch precious meat to feed as many people as possible. At least tonight, there'd be plenty of food to go around.

They've been cooking this way "on the Island" for centuries, but most of The Guys' recipes come from Jorge and Raul's mothers. They are family recipes that The Guys brought north to feed a city hungry for a taste of home. Once the tamales were cooking, the ladies swept into the kitchen to fix up the rest of the meal.

The food was delicious: savory and spicy, but not hot. The meats and peppers danced a perfect salsa together. Steak, Cuban sandwiches, picadillo, and of course our tamales. We all laughed and drank and devoured our Latin feast. I was officially done working and started saying goodbye, but The Guys made it clear the party was just starting.

The men moved to the pool, and we dangled our feet in the deep end while the women cleaned up. Raul brought out some excellent cigars and Jorge pulled out the rum. Clearly, we weren't going anywhere. I looked at the cigar Raul had given me.

"Cuban?"

"What do you think?" He lit up and inhaled deeply.

"Not a bad way to spend your birthday, huh Raul? What were birthdays like in Cuba?"

"I don't remember much. But I do know that I spent the night of my twenty-first birthday in Castro's jail for speaking out against the Revolution. I was there for a while . . . "

"I spent my twenty-first birthday at a backyard surprise party, then I drove off in the car my parents gave me to meet friends at a downtown blues bar." Raul just smiled.

"In Cuba, you cannot talk against, you cannot criticize Castro. In public no one will say anything, but in private . . . "

He told me about a country with a 99 percent literacy rate, unable to feed its babies. He told me about a country raped by its leaders, abandoned by its neighbors, and impoverished by fascism. He told me how, as a young man, he realized the only way to save his country would be to destroy it. As part of an entire generation of men whose only hope for survival was to engineer the extinction of their leader, he was defeated and forced to retreat . . . for now. The weight of that retreat is written on the face of every Cuban in Miami. They

> **But behind the smiles there always lurks a thick curtain of sadness. It's what binds them all together, neighbor or not. They're all here because of the same heartache.**

don't miss an opportunity to have a laugh, but behind the smiles there always lurks a thick curtain of sadness. It's what binds them all together, neighbor or not. They're all here because of the same heartache.

I asked him why the Cubans stay in Miami. Once they fight through the Coast Guard and the Beach Police and touch dry land, they are automatically granted asylum. Why not fan out and assimilate into other parts of the country? He looked at me like I was loco.

"Because we're going back. We are waiting for the day when we can return to our home and rebuild what he destroyed."

"Well, I can understand that," I said. "America's no paradise. Between the selfish crooks in Washington, and the selfish crooks on Wall Street, poverty, racism, greed . . . sometimes I think I should become a refugee myself."

Raul stared at me through the haze, and pointed with his cigar.

"You have no idea how privileged you are. America is our beacon, everyone's beacon. A place where freedom is written into law and power changes every four years at the whim of the people. Without bloodshed. Without fail."

"Or not," I cynically remarked. "Remember Florida in 2000?"

"Yes I do. You voted, there were questions, but nobody died. On the television, people were accusing the government, the governor, of fraud . . . yet no protestor went to jail. And in the end, the rule of law was applied and eventually prevailed," he whispered. "I'll always remember Florida."

And so will I.

As the red Florida sun dropped through Jorge's palm trees, I leaned back in his pool and realized I was finally satisfied. After four hundred cities, thousands of miles, and over a thousand delicious meals, the most American person I met turned out to be from someplace else.

Like us all. Even the Native Americans started out on a different continent and walked on water to get to the promised land. Since the pre-dawn of time, something has drawn people to our big plot of dirt. But what?

Sitting at Mallory Square all those months ago, I assumed that by the time we were done, all my questions would be answered. That walking the walk while talking would paint one, cohesive definitive "America." But all I ended up with was a book full of seemingly unrelated snapshots, some blurry, others cropped all wrong, yet all equally real. Sitting in front of another South Florida sunset, I realized I was back to square one.

Until the Cubans, foreigners here against their will and completely by choice, brought my images into focus.

We're a country of optimists. Regardless of where we came from or when, we were convinced from afar that America would be better. And even at the points in our history when it clearly wasn't, enough of us held onto that belief to survive and make it so once again.

Especially in Domino Park where fleeting conflicts always pale to shared political passions. All over the park, I watched as men stood, spoke and pointed south, and even though I understand virtually no Spanish, I knew exactly what they were talking about.

Freedom. The only reason they'd left their island paradise. On boats, on doors, in '57 Chevys, they risked their lives, left their families, and fought their way onto our shores to become part of our grand experiment. Because even without TV, newspapers, or mail, they knew with Freedom, everything else is possible.

It's the only thing we all share. The freedom to drive from Miami to Seattle and listen to whatever you want to along the way, as long as you can name the artist, album, and exact song title. If you want to stop for a square dance in Little Rock, you can. If you want to drink some whiskey with a radical, no one will stop you. If you want to pull off for some chili in Wyoming, you might get some company, but one way or another, you'll get a mouthful.

As I finish writing this book today, the time for my spring ritual has come around again. After my car is packed, gassed, GPS'd, and iPodded, I'll pause before turning the key, like I've done almost every March 22 since 1986, to read what is, for my money, the best opening paragraph in American letters:

> *When I was young and the urge to be someplace else was on me, I was assured by mature people that maturity would cure this itch. . . . Now that I am fifty-eight perhaps senility will do the job. Nothing has worked. Four hoarse blasts of a ship's whistle still raise the hair on my neck and set my feet to tapping. The sound of a jet, an engine warming up, even the clopping of shod hooves on pavement brings on the ancient shudder, the dry mouth and vacant eye, the hot palms and the churn of stomach high up under the rib cage. . . . I fear the disease is incurable.*

—John Steinbeck, *Travels with Charley,* 1960

PAULA APRIL'S NEW ORLEANS–STYLE BREAD PUDDING

2 cups bread cubes
2 cups milk

3 tablespoons butter

¼ cup sugar

2 eggs

Dash of salt

½ teaspoon vanilla

1. Use old bread, crusts and all, cutting it into ¼-inch cubes. Place in buttered 1-quart baking dish. Scald the milk with the butter and sugar.
2. Slightly beat the eggs; add the salt; then stir in the warm milk, add vanilla. Pour over bread cubes—make sure you cover the bread cubes, leaving just a few points showing, so they can soak it all up.
3. Set the baking dish in a pan of warm water up to the level of the pudding and bake at 350°F for about an hour or until a small knife comes out clean when inserted in the center.

Now for the good part:

You can add raisins, any kind of chopped nuts, 1 can of crushed pineapple, 1 can of fruit cocktail (less the juice), coconut, chocolate chips, craisins or any variety of such, or just about anything else you want in there. Paula also adds cinnamon, nutmeg, and more sugar depending on what other stuff she adds.

Any kind of bread will do: white, wheat, sourdough, biscuits, doughnuts, plain cake . . . whatever you've got lying around. This is a recycling project!

That's the recipe as Paula sent it to me. However, I happen to know that when we cooked it on camera, there was one other ingredient in there: BOURBON.

You can use any bourbon you like, just make sure you use enough of it. What's enough. . . . who's to say. But you'll know if you add too much.

Enjoy!

FRIED GREEN TOMATOES

Use only under-ripe, green tomatoes.

1. In an iron skillet heat vegetable oil until it pops.
2. Slice green tomatoes ¼-inch thick and dip in egg yolk.
3. Rub tomato slices in a mix of bread crumbs, salt, and pepper, until they're coated well on both sides.
4. Fry until golden brown.

THREE GUYS FROM MIAMI: TAMALES DE CARNE DE CERDO

Cuban Pork Tamales

1½ pounds pork in chunks

Pinch of salt

Water to cover meat

2 whole peeled garlic cloves

1 tablespoon vinegar

3 cups fresh or frozen corn

¾ cup lard, butter, or shortening

2½ cups chicken broth

2½ cups masa harina (a finely ground corn flour used for tamales)

1 teaspoon Bijol powder for color (or substitute annatto seed oil or powder)

2 cups finely chopped onion

2 cups finely chopped green pepper

Olive oil for sautéing

5 cloves garlic, minced

½ (6-ounce) can tomato paste

½ cup warm water

½ cup red or white wine

Juice of 1 large lemon

1 teaspoon salt

½ teaspoon freshly ground black pepper

Corn husks (soak dried cornhusks in hot water
   before using)

Note: For meat, you need pork with plenty of fat—either well marbled or with a fat layer or both. We've had good luck with de-boned country style pork ribs or a pork shoulder roast.

1. Cut the pork up into smaller pieces—no more than 2 inches thick and about 3 inches long. Add a pinch of salt and place in a 3-quart saucepan. Add water to just barely cover the meat. Add garlic cloves and vinegar. Bring to a boil, reduce heat to low, and simmer, uncovered, until all of the water has boiled away. Be sure to keep an eye on it! This process will render some of the fat out of the meat.

2. Fry the pork pieces in this rendered fat just until lightly brown but not too crispy! The meat should be tender and stringy. Remove the meat. Trim off any excess fat (there shouldn't be any), and break up the meat into small shreds.

3. Slice the corn kernels off a cob of fresh sweet corn until you have 3 cups (or use frozen corn). Quickly grind the corn in a food processor with your choice of fat (lard, butter, or

shortening) until you get a very coarse mixture with visible corn kernels. Don't over-process!

4. Remove the corn from the processor and place in a large 8-quart stockpot. Blend in 2½ cups warm chicken broth and 2 cups masa harina to the ground corn. Add the Bijol powder (or annatto) to give it a nice yellow color.

5. Sauté the onion and green pepper in olive oil at medium heat, stirring occasionally, until the onions are soft. Add garlic and continue to sauté for 2 to 3 minutes. Do not drain off excess oil! Mix tomato paste in warm water and add it and the wine to the vegetables. Simmer for about 10 minutes.

6. Add the pork and vegetable mixture to the corn mixture in the stockpot. Add lemon juice, salt, and pepper, and stir. Cook the mixture on low heat, stirring frequently (don't let it burn!) until it thickens—about 20 minutes. Add more masa as necessary to make a stiff but pliable paste. Taste and add salt if needed. Remove from heat and let cool.

7. To make the tamales, take 2 corn husks and place them flat on a cutting board, overlapping the widest parts of the husk to create a pocket for the filling. Put some of the meat and corn mixture in the center of the husks. Fold the husks over the filling the short way, and then fold the long way from the ends. Tie with a string.

8. Tamales are best cooked in a large pot with about 2 inches of water in the bottom. If you have the little insert that keeps the food off the bottom, great! Add the tamales, standing them on end, and cover the pot. Bring the water to a boil and cover. Reduce heat to low and simmer/steam about 90 minutes to 2 hours.

Important: Be sure to check the water level occasionally so that the pot doesn't run dry!

Tip: Freshly cooked tamales will be a bit mushy. The best way to make tamales is to cook them a day ahead and then put them in the refrigerator overnight. Cooling helps the tamales firm up to the proper consistency. The next day, just steam them long enough to heat through. If you'd like to make a large batch and freeze them, always cook the tamales first and then freeze. Usually we can't resist and end up eating a couple of "loose" tamales the same day!

Makes about 18 to 24 medium-size tamales.

Recipe and editorial content from the book:
Three Guys From Miami Cook Cuban
Gibbs Smith Publisher, Copyright 2004
Used by permission.

COURTESY OF THREE GUYS FROM MIAMI/NANCY BUNDT

ACKNOWLEDGMENTS

A big thank you to all our cooks, their families, and friends. Thanks for welcoming us into your worlds and showing us the times of our lives. We really enjoyed your company—except for the one dufus in Cincinnati.

Though it may have looked like it on TV, I did not make my journey alone. The fun and adventure would not have been possible without the help, support, and talents of an army of experts:

The people at Film Garden who Googled, planned, booked (and rebooked) every mile, especially Judy and Beau. They found us the best places to visit and the best people to cook . . . with.

Our Travel Channel exec, David Gerber—an executive who has no idea what a TV executive is supposed to do. Instead, he spent his time making good suggestions, previewing material, and letting us keep jokes we loved, even when he didn't.

The literati at Globe Pequot Press for making my show into a book. Heather, Mary, Julie, and Joshua. You helped me preserve the fruit and toss out the rind as painlessly as possible.

Nadine on Southwest for hands down, the most intentionally hilarious cabin safety lecture ever.

Sharlene Martin for dotting all the t's and continually explaining to me that writing a book is different than making TV.

Ginny Wiessman for taking a real interest in my first play when I was in 6th grade and caring enough to tell me all the reasons my characters stunk and my jokes weren't funny. And then suggesting ways, if I was really serious about being a writer, to make it better.

My dad for refusing to buy me a typewriter and insisting I learn to use a computer. My brothers for being my first, and best, audience.

My Crew: Floyd, Eddie, Mike, and Stephanie for doing all the hard work. Libby and Pam for doing all the easy work—while taking most of the entertaining photographs in this book. Tom, Shooter, Hiroki, the guys who got tangled in their cords, and especially Brian Miller for keeping all things always in focus . . . with lemon.

You, for reading this book and supporting me in my circuitous road to wherever it is I'm headed. Now put it down, get off your ass, and make your own memories.

Index

About the Author

Mark DeCarlo has been a comedian, host, producer, and actor since becoming the all-time champion on NBC's *Sale of the Century,* three months after his graduation from UCLA. He hasn't had a real job since.

He is also a cartoon voice actor, best known as the voice of Hugh Neutron (Jimmy's dad) on Nickelodeon's hit series, *Jimmy Neutron, Boy Genius.* Mark appears regularly on radio stations across the country—most notably in his hometown of Chicago on Steve Cochran's WGN Radio show, talking food, travel, and funny.

Mark hosted four seasons of the popular TV show *Taste of America* (2005–2008), following multi-season runs on *The X Show, Sunday Dinner,* and the FOX dating show, *Studs.* As an actor, he's appeared on shows such as *Seinfeld* and *Curb Your Enthusiasm* and in films such as *Buffy the Vampire Slayer* and *Mobsters and Mormons.*

His new series, *EconomicalECO,* is a humorous look at Eco Living . . . for the 97 percent of the country that doesn't gobble granola and live in a yurt. Mark continues to travel the country, performing comedy and music and eating the best food he can find. When he's not on the road, Mark and his Cubana amore live in the Hollywood Hills in an energy-efficient eco-house . . . with a big-screen TV.

Stay current on Mark's meanderings at his Web site: www.markdecarlo.com.